HOT WAR, COLD WAR & BEYOND

TALES FROM THE TRENCHES OF THE 20TH CENTURY

The Memoirs of Austin Goodrich

Austin Goodrich

iUniverse, Inc.
Bloomington

HOT WAR, COLD WAR & BEYOND Tales from the Trenches of the 20th Century
The Memoirs of Austin Goodrich

iUniverse books may be ordered through booksellers or by contacting:

iUniverse
1663 Liberty Drive
Bloomington, IN 47403
www.iuniverse.com
1-800-Authors (1-800-288-4677)

ISBN: 978-1-4502-9578-9 (pbk)
ISBN: 978-1-4502-9579-6 (ebk)

Printed in the United States of America

iUniverse rev. date: 2/21/2011

This memoir is dedicated with love and gratitude to my children – Britt, Kristina, Austin Jay, Timo and Samantha – who enriched my life beyond measure. Also to my loving sisters – Helen, Eleanor and Ethel. With thanks for the memories!

Introduction

In the middle of my eighth decade on Planet Earth I embarked on a trip down memory lane that kept me seated in slumped solitude staring at an empty computer monitor screen for months in search of a purposeful path to pursue. It was like sorting through the contents of a garbage truck in search of an apple core that I had thrown away with only a single bite taken out of it. Finally, I decided to end my fruitless search by using the word *apple* itself as the first alphabetical guidepost on a meandering 85-year-old's trip back down memory lane. I was amazed at how the letters of the alphabet gave rise to words which spawned memories of living through the years of the Great Depression that we refused to acknowledge, and the Second World War that pushed us onto the main stage of our shrunken world in the Cold War. If you'd care to join me, fasten your seat belts for a multi-generational ride through a century that may well have moved faster and in more directions than all of the history that preceded it.

In the interest of putting my recollections into perspective and reducing the cloud of unrealism produced by the sentiment of age, I have included some contemporary observations supplied by some of my children, for none of which I will accept any responsibility. After all, it's my rear view window, not theirs.

Bon voyage!

A is for Apple

Apples played a major role in my life that began on August 30, 1925. There were two kinds in my particular world: Big red, sweet *Delicious* apples that we kids just loved to eat, and *Macintosh* apples that were small and face-grimacing sour, but with lots of flavor. Big, sweet green apples called Granny Smith came later and had to be bought at the grocery store when our parents could afford them or at the Farmers' Market that stood on a concrete slab that covered half a city block in the southeast corner of Battle Creek's downtown, and was open on Saturdays only.

The largest apple tree in the neighborhood stood in the yard at the south end of Elizabeth Street separated from Sherman Road by a vacant lot owned by someone who managed to hold on to it despite the financial pressures of the Great Depression. We kids knew just about every homeowner on the two-block street except for the ladies who lived in the house with the crabapple tree. They didn't have any children, but they were okay, because they never said anything to us about our scurrying about like monkeys in their huge tree. It was a great climbing tree with branches that spread all over the place, and for a few weeks in the fall it provided us with sour little crabapples that made our eyes squint up tight when we ate them. Still, if you could get by that first bitter flavor these little apples left your mouth with a fresh taste that triggered the urge to fling what was left of the little fruit at a buddy seated on a branch down below. Invariably, this signaled the start of a crabapple war.

One day the game came to an abrupt end when a misguided piece of fruit struck and hit an upstairs window in the nice ladies' bedroom. It may not have been the shot heard round the world but it instantly signaled the immediate departure of the young poachers from their perches in the gnarled branches of the crabapple tree. The errant shot might have broken the window, but nobody paused to check. It was generally agreed that the crabapples were getting too ripe and sour anyway, and maybe we just ought to wait 'til next fall to resume our crabapple war.

Road Apples is what we called the light brown balls left in the street in the trail of horse-drawn wagons that delivered ice and groceries to the residents of Elizabeth Street. These decidedly inedible brown spheres were studiously ignored by all humanoids but somehow attracted the appetites of sparrows and small dogs, which had to be chased away from them. For some reason we never could figure out, dogs seemed to be attracted to these ugly droppings and if left alone would take a taste or two from the street platter or, more disgustingly, roll in the equine excrement. By unwritten but strictly enforced neighborhood law, it was considered a prime duty of all young street police to remove this disgusting sight by chasing off dogs from their street leftovers whenever possible. If we reached the scene too late, it was the duty of the boy whose family owned the dog to scrub clean his pet's malodorous coat.

A is for America
By Britt Vesla Weaver

I've always loved the way that America the word itself, rolls off the tongue. America starts and ends with a soft *a,* the sound of calming chants. "America!" the word itself is so lyrical that it begs to be sung.

Growing up overseas shaped my notions of America. The country was big and everything in it was big, really big. Big winged cars, big apples, big stores, big yards, big crayon boxes, and big highways. The experience called America dwarfed the European countries I lived in. Returning from America to Norway, Finland, Sweden Holland or Germany was like taking a shrinking pill – the world became more petite, more scrunched.

America meant all things new: new houses, new schools, new movies, new cereals, and so many new ice cream flavors. I learned new games, like Hula Hoop and Bingo. American music burst out of the radio in new, exciting patterns, with new hits every month. With practice I finally perfected the art of finger snapping to the big new sound of rock 'n' roll. And I learned to whistle the new tunes, which was even better. But nothing beat American television for sheer novelty. It took my breath away with its seemingly endless stream of new stories every day. Just as interesting to my impressionable European mind were the commercials. I watched, fascinated, as products (always new and improved) flashed across the screen and it became my mission to convince Mama to buy all of them.

I lapped up all this bigness and newness with relish.

My cousin, Austin, and his mom and dad once came for a visit to our brand new home in McLean, Virginia, when I was six. Cousin Aust was only a little older than me, but that was enough to make him and anything he did a big deal. He pulled out a crayon case that must have boasted 200 colors, all stacked in neat rows, with the tips pointing up. I was fascinated. I had never realized there were so many colors in existence, and that each had a place next to another one that was similar, but not the same. I hated that he had this case and I didn't. I just knew that he owned the Crayola set because he was more American than I was and I wondered if I would become American enough to one day possess such a magnificent set.

One of these days I'm going to buy the biggest box of crayons made.

B is for Britt

No question about it, your first-born child is special. Will it be a boy or a girl? What color eyes will it have? (Mine were brown, my wife Vesla's were blue.) What shall we call it? My first choice for a boy baby was "Bruce" to honor the memory of my company commander Captain Bruce Macalester, who was shot and killed in the final week of World War II. That had to be dismissed to avoid the baby being saddled with a name pronounced like "brus," the Norwegian word for soda pop. We could just hear the baby's Norwegian grandparents greeting their grandson with the equivalent of "How is our little Pepsi today? So the choice of a boy's name was put off until further notice while we settled on a girl's name, which was easy. We both loved the name Britt, the name of Vesla's niece, who used the nickname Bibi, so we decided to name our daughter "Britt Vesla Goodrich."

She arrived early on the morning of January 15th at St. Eriks Sjukhus in Stockholm, Sweden. Her dad was at her mama's bedside throughout the 22-hour labor except for a short visit home for a change of clothes and a bite to eat. The doctor in attendance was a stranger to us but he did a fine job as could be expected of any well-trained medical doctor. The only problem was Vesla's assignment to share a room with a woman who it so happened had just lost her baby in giving birth. Every time our healthy baby was brought into the room, Vesla's roommate understandably burst into tears. With this experience in mind, we opted to have all three of our younger children delivered in private hospitals (Kristina in Stockholm, Austin Jay in Helsinki, Finland and Timothy Lance in The Hague, Netherlands.) The latter private-pay offspring were delivered, housed and cared for at a charge of about a quarter of what it costs to have a baby in the United States. All of them stayed with their mom in a hospital during their first week in their strange new environment.

They were all bald redheads-to-be but that's where the similarity ended. Their different personalities made each one of them special and especially loved.

It was about a year later that Britt returned to a Swedish hospital under circumstances that can best be described as traumatic both for her and her parents. It was after a long (pre-jet) Pan Am DC-6 flight from New York to Oslo that had to be diverted due to weather several hundred miles east to Stockholm, Sweden. During the flight, Britt developed a cough and respiratory problems, which we hoped a few hours rest in a Stockholm hotel would relieve. A doctor summoned to the hotel gave her a medication and approved our continued travel back to Oslo via the night train. Unfortunately, her respiratory problem persisted and the Swedish State Railways conductor somehow was able to summon a physician to come aboard at a small station the name of which I've forgotten, to examine our little daughter. He gave her a medication and got the conductor to call ahead to make arrangements for our little girl to be taken to a hospital in Karlstad at around 2 in the morning. Britt's mother, Eva , nicknamed "Vesla" and I bundled our one-year-old daughter in a Swedish State Railways blanket as the train came to a stop at deserted Karlstad Station.

With a tight hold on our precious daughter I leaped off the train, sprinted across a platform and jumped into a taxi waiting on the street. We sped at breakneck speed through the darkened streets of Karlstad to the hospital Emergency entrance where a nurse hurriedly led the way to a small treatment room down the hall. There a doctor in street clothes stood holding a gauze dressing in one hand and a bottle of ether in the other. I followed the doctor's order to lay Britt down and hold her head steady while he in one swift motion poured s large splash of ether on the dressing, which he held over Britt's nose to put her to sleep and then swiftly cut a slit at the base of her throat to expose her wind pipe. Another quick scalpel move and there was created a small opening for the insertion of a metal device that gave access to the clogged wind pipe. Under the doctor's direction, two nurses who had run into the emergency room with a noisy pump device used it to remove the grey slime that had clogged Britt's wind pipe. I saw in a terrible moment that the color and smile had been drained from the face of our baby. As I silently, fervently whispered for God's help, the Swedish medical team inserted a hose into the wound to allow oxygen to reach into our little girl's lungs.

She was put to bed with one of her hands held firmly in mine, while the other was loosely bound to a bed railing with gauze to prevent her from getting at the foreign object inserted into her throat. Every so often the pump would switch on to perform its noisy, scary, life-saving work, and a nurse appeared to make sure that it was working properly. During this procedure it was my terrible loving duty to hold Britt's small hands in my own. By mid-morning of the following day the acute, life-threatening danger that croup had posed to Britt's life had passed, and I was able to call her mom, Vesla, with the good news. Then it was her turn to open the tearful floodgates of grateful joy.

A few days later, we brought our daughter to her grandparents' home on a hillside overlooking Oslo Fjord where we went out on the veranda to contemplate the awesome sight of a million lights twinkling below in celebration of the birth of Jesus Christ. And the life of our beloved daughter, Britt Vesla Goodrich.

Amen.

B Is For Beer

Elsewhere in our world, beer is consumed as a beverage to lend taste and a measure of good humor to a meal served after noon, except in European train stations where it is served and drunk at any time of the night or day. Only in America are people under the age of 21 forbidden by law to purchase or to savor this ancient beverage in public. Perhaps it's the work of our puritan ancestors who limited the consumption of beer to private homes lest we put our fun-loving instincts on public display. In any case, beer was certainly a staple in the liquid diet of young people where I spent my teen years growing up in Battle Creek, Michigan.

Food City Beer was brewed in Battle Creek and was a favorite among the youth who lived there because of its cheap price. But as soon as we could afford to buy national brands our taste buds turned to Detroit-brewed *Stroh's* and the more exotic Milwaukee beers produced across the big lake. *Schlitz* was a favorite followed by the socially pretentious *Miller High Life,* which was priced a few pennies a bottle beyond the range of most teenagers.

Budweiser, named after a Czechoslovakian pilsner brewed in St. Louis, was popular even though it was priced a few cents more than the Milwaukee brands. We quaffed most of our suds in or near our cars parked on an undeveloped parcel of land known as the Tower, presumably because it was on high ground that commanded a view of roads leading up to it that might be used by police patrol cars. Police never bothered us anyway, probably because they preferred to let us stay in locations on the edge of town rather than wasting gas in futile searches for us closer to our homes, where only God knows what we might be up to. After all, necking and beer-drinking were not ranked high on the list of social activities demanding police attention in those good old days.

When cold weather put a cap on most after-hours traffic at the Tower, some of us found warmth in a small bar behind the Security National Bank building that had served as a speakeasy during the Prohibition years. The place still had an unused pool table whose green felt was stained with spilled beer and God know what else, and was still run by a squatty, aproned bartender named Otto Gempsch. Half of the view through the large front window was obscured by a dark green curtain suspended on brass rings. Women looking for their husbands in the darkened interior had to jump to get a look inside, staging a payday ballet that was studiously ignored by the saloon's regulars for more than a decade.

Otto looked on his young customers with ill-concealed contempt, but accepted their coin almost without question. An exception to his no-questions-asked hospitality occurred one night when a high school customer of diminutive stature named Bob Roelof reached up to drop a coin on the bar and squeaked out "Gimme a short beer, Otto." Whereupon the proprietor looked down at the boy who would later become a leading dentist in the city and replied "I'll give ya a short trip to the front door, is what I'll give ya." And out he went. It was the only known instance when Otto's business sense was trumped by his need to maintain a measure of respect for the state's legal drinking age of twenty-one.

A few years later, at about the time when our teen genes began to focus on the fair sex (none of whom ever entered Otto's establishment), we gravitated to hangouts beyond the city limits where age limits were never enforced. One friendly roadhouse served beer in pitchers and featured live music on weekend evenings. There my steady and I used to snuggle down in a booth with a pitcher of suds with occasional flings on the dance floor. We usually shared our booth with older but still young people, who thought we were a married couple. We didn't deny it, and in fact got a huge kick out of playing the charade all evening. Maybe that special pleasure derived from living a little lie contributed to the special delight that life under an assumed identity as a case officer for the Central Intelligence Agency provided me in later years. Who knows?

Another favorite site for Saturday night in our teens was a restaurant and dance hall named La Belle located on Gull Lake about a 12-mile drive from both Battle Creek to the east and Kalamazoo to the west. The place was graced with a friendly bartender, who on slow evenings was known to help his young patrons with their high school algebra. And the band directed by a fellow named King was a cut above any live music we had ever heard before. The beer was a bit more expensive, but you could still get a pitcher for a dollar and a quarter that included a tip for the waiter. I can only remember one bad encounter at La Belle.

It occurred during the war when as 20-year-olds in uniform a few of us were refused entry on the grounds of our being a year short of the 21-year-old age limit. To compound this insult, the checker was himself a moonlighting serviceman. Needless to say, he only lasted in his power position for a week.

B Is For Blackball

Jumping forward into the post-WW II years for a moment, I recall an incident that produced an indelible impression on my way of thinking about a lot of things. You might say it produced in me a democratic mind set, even though I have mostly voted in general elections for the Republican Party's slate of candidates. The setting for this event was a general meeting of the Psi Upsilon fraternity brothers in our club room at 1000 Hill Street in Ann Arbor, Michigan. We were all dressed in our black gowns seated in single rows along the walls, with our elected officers seated on raised thrones at the end of the room, which was never used for any other official purpose than for these fraternity chapter meetings. (Unofficially, the room served as the site for occasional illicit romps with co-eds or, more frequently, with local girls seeking non-academic encounters with students enrolled under the G.I. Bill of Rights.)

After singing frat songs and attending to some routine matters, the meeting was thrown open on one occasion for the discussion of new business and I addressed the brothers with a proposal that I had considered for some time and which I thought would be approved by my fraternity brothers in the interest of common sense and fair play. I was sorely mistaken. We were to consider candidates to *pledge* for membership in our "Greek" fraternity located in a prestigious location on Hill St. just a black south of the Law campus and another block from the Literature, Science and the Arts and Engineering schools. This fraternity was one of the most respected houses on the campus and included on its among its members a U.S. President, Chester Arthur, and other notables in the academic, sports and business worlds.

Normally, pledge candidates recommended by a screening committee were accepted after a routine procedure in which a box was passed and members could drop into it a white ball (for a yea vote) or a black ball (for a nay vote). One black ball was all that was needed to prevent a candidate for membership to be pledged. For the first time in my memory, a black ball was cast to block from membership a pimply-faced bespectacled student who had to be considered because he was the son of a Phi chapter brother living in Chicago.

I was shocked by the prospect that the future of this boy (he was too young to have served as most of us had, in WWII) could be seriously damaged by his being denied the possibility of following in his father's college footsteps. I rose to plead his cause, citing the history of the black ball, which was adopted when fraternities consisted of handful of members living in close quarters. In that context it was understandable that if a single member could not live with a person for whatever reason, he should have the right to exclude the boy from membership. But with three dozen "brothers" living in the same house, it was unfair and unrealistic to maintain this exclusivity. Despite my plea on his behalf the boy was *blackballed*, denied membership in our elitist club.

A few months later, I left my quarters in the house (a living room and bedroom suite shared with a brother and kept clean by a Negro servant) and moved into a bed-and-bath arrangement in a private home. I explained that my move was necessitated by financial reasons. As some of my closer Psi U friends knew, that was only a part, and a small part at that, of my real motivation for moving back into the social mainstream where I suppose I've always felt more comfortable.

C Is For Childhood Fun and Games

Yes, dear readers, there has to be a connection between our youthful experiences and the paths we followed into life as grown-ups, but be warned that shared experiences in our young days seldom lead to identical or even similar lives as adults. So far as I know, I'm the only member of my childhood society to get into the secret world of the Central Intelligence Agency in my adult years. But it can't be denied that the experiences of my youth may have somehow laid the groundwork for my move into the world of secrecy and make-believe as an adult. First let's fast forward for a peek at my current scene.

A beautiful new playground for young children has been constructed in a park two blocks from where I live the good life of a CIA retiree in Port Washington, Wisconsin, just half an hour north of Milwaukee. Here safety issues are paramount. At the entrance to a new playground, are posted a list of more than a dozen rules governing use of the completely fenced enclosure and a heated indoor toilet and changing facility attached to it. The kids have to be accompanied by adults at all times, of course, and never are they permitted to bring their pets with them into the playground.

As a matter of fact, unleashed dogs are not permitted in the park or any place else in the city. I have personally granted "Arrow," my Brittany Spaniel named for the arrowhead-shaped white mark on the top of his head, an age-related exemption to this rule. At first the local police objected to Arrow's running free, but when they realized that I had no intention of leashing him, they gave up and made friends with this dog who helped them enforce the park's 20 mph speed limit by threatening to run in front of any car exceeding this limit.

In marked contrast to the closely regulated and supervised situation of modern play areas for pre-teens, the places where kids of my vintage played were totally devoid of adult presence. We devised, managed and refereed our fun and games on our own. Adults were not actually banned from participating in or attending our games. It was just that we didn't need or want them around. They had their games: golf, tennis. bridge, gin rummy, whatever. We had ours: baseball, football, pom-pom-pullaway and a dozen varieties of tag, including two-hands-below-the-belt and squat tag. (As much as I dislike modern play grounds and ball parks built and managed by adults, I have to admit that the current shortage of vacant lots sadly limits the areas available for kids to manage their own fun and games.)

Our games differed from adult games in a couple of respects important to the process of democratic problem-solving. This started with the choice of game to be played. First there were certain natural factors at work determining this choice. In winter, you have to have ice to play ice hockey (substituting tree limbs for manufactured sticks of which we had only a few), but no sticks are needed to play pom-pom-pullaway on ice or relay races on ice that circled the island at the lagoon, where there was a cozy warmed place to change into your skates without danger of anyone taking your street shoes or galoshes that were stored there.

In spring, fall and summer the choices were largely limited by the number of players available. You really needed to have at least ten players to have two five-boy teams for baseball or football, but you could play baseball with four on each team if the team at bat supplied a catcher. If fewer athletes were available, you could play move-up baseball, where you moved from the outfield to the infield to pitcher to catcher and finally to the batter's box where you remained until you struck out, were thrown out or were disabled by one of Austin's wild submarine pitches.

With more than a dozen players on hand we were able to choose up sides, which involved advanced rules-making not governed by Roberts Rules of Order. First choice was usually awarded by tossing the bat up with the two captains, the two best players, grabbing for the first choice. Then it had to be decided whether or not to allow a crab claw (fist) to be used to go over the bottom of the bat handle, which was at the top of the tossed bat, to get the first choice.

In football, the process was usually simplified with a coin toss, or a rock pitched to a line in the dirt. Of course, during or after the selection process, the captains could make personnel trades that sometimes involved one side giving up a highly-skilled specialist (a punter, passer or receiver) to get *two* players in return. It was all a part of applying democratic principles to gain a tactical edge. Sound a bit like the tactics employed today in business, politics, life in general? Well, it was just that.

C Is For Construction (for kids)

In addition to providing space for ball fields, vacant lots created by the development of new neighborhoods also spawned the construction of small-scale habitats for the exclusive use of all the kids who could fit inside them. New buildings always left scrap pieces of lumber for the neighborhood children to pick up after sunset. These materials were quickly put to use in the construction of a boys-only club house near, but not *too* near, the new house construction site. When available, the new residence was covered with a coat of tar paper and a small entrance measuring a foot by two feet was covered by a scrap of old carpeting. The place was strictly off limits to adults, but Mrs. Geyer apparently hadn't gotten the message when she one Saturday morning got down at the entrance to inquire about the whereabouts of her son, Carl.

"Not in here," came the unanimous response from within. Whereupon Mrs. Geyer made the mistake of lifting the rug curtain for a look inside and was met by a cloud of Bull Durham rolled cigarette smoke that knocked her back onto her amply cushioned posterior. Never to return to the kids-only club house.

To maintain fair play and orderly behavior inside our huts it was necessary to make and enforce rules of behavior. First of all, loud voices had to b ruled out lest they draw unwanted attention to our presence and what we were up to. Secondly, the close quarters of the hut demanded that rules against farting be enforced most rigorously. This was easy when the emission of a malodorous gas was accompanied by a distinctive rattling noise that immediately identified the culprit, who became subjected to a deserved beating about his shoulders by his peers. The judicial process was complicated, however, when an anonymous farter cut a so-called *silent defender*. When any hut dweller first detected the smell he had to immediately place his index finger to the side of his nose and emit a short whistle. As the other boys saw this signal they quickly followed suit. The culprit was identified without any further judicial process as the last person to exercise the finger-to-nose-whistle signal. He was immediately found guilty of farting and subjected to a hammering about his arms and shoulders. This procedure may have lacked judicial merit, but the boys all agreed that someone had to be punished, whether guilty as sin or innocent as an angel.

C Is for CIA and Cover

There are many kinds of cover. There's the soft green cover for a comforter constructed on a wooden frame set up in our living room by my mother, grandmother and aunts that I slept under from the age of two until I left for college fifteen years later. Then there's the cover I used to conceal from public view my professional career as a staff agent in the Central Intelligence Agency, the CIA, for short. That's the kind I'll talk about here and now.

In the spring of 1949, I was about to graduate from the University of Michigan with a BA (for Bullshit Anonymous) degree, and our family was about to take a vacation in Washington, DC. Thoughts of getting a job crossed my mind occasionally, but seldom upset my concentration on the pleasures of college life centered on the consumption of beer at the Pretzel Bell tavern in downtown Ann Arbor, where I held the record for table-to-table emptying of a glass of draft beer (1.1 sec).

Since beer-guzzling was not considered an appropriate career, the thought crept into my mind that I might try to line up a government job during our forthcoming family vacation. I asked my poly-sci teacher if he thought I might be able to get a job in the field of foreign affairs. This would get me into an area where I could best carry out my secret pledge made in combat to devote my life to the cause of world peace. He said he had heard they were hiring at the recently established Central Intelligence Agency, and suggested that I give them a call and mention his name. So after attending the signing of the North Atlantic Treaty (using a letter from my local newspaper editor for admission) I opened the phone book to CIA and dialed their number. I said I was about to graduate from college and I'd like to talk with someone about getting a job. Could I come by your office? Sure could. I was given an address at a Naval Hospital near the Lincoln Memorial, where I was invited to come around for an interview the following morning, which I did.

A nice lady met me at the door, and led me into a small cubicle where I was given some application forms to fill out. When she returned, she asked me what I thought the CIA did. I gave the poly-sci 101 answer: CIA collected and processed intelligence for the government to use in formulating an executing our foreign policy. She then asked if research and analysis of intelligence would be my chief interest, and I answered that actually I'd like to get into something a little more active, maybe get involved in work overseas. This seemed to please her, and she asked if I could return the following morning to talk with a man who might be able to offer me aposition. I said my family had planned to return home, but I'd see if we could stay over another day and I'd let her know later in the afternoon.

My dad, had not planned to extend our visit to Washington, and I later learned he had no additional funds in those pre-credit card days to do so. But when I mentioned that staying an extra day might lead to solid employment for me, he readily agreed to postpone our departure. He didn't tell any of the rest of the family about the change in plans, but they went along with the revised schedule even though it meant we'd have to cut a day from the scheduled time it would take to get home. God bless 'em.

So I returned the following morning to meet the late Frank Wisner, a senior CIA ops officer, who had served with Bill Colby and many other CIA officers in the wartime OSS (Office of Strategic Services). He told me CIA would have a job for me, but regretfully added that it would take about 90 days to process my security clearance. (Thanks to high speed computers the process now takes twice that long) If I could take some sort of short-term employment, they'd give me a call when my clearance was done and I could come to Washington to start work. Fair enough, I said, and a hand-shake sealed the deal that would provide me with the opportunity to serve my country, mostly under deep cover, for the next quarter of a century.

In preparation for setting up a stay-behind network for activation in WW III, I was extremely fortunate to have as my boss Bill Colby, who had served with the OSS and had parachuted into occupied France and Germany to work with resistance groups. This bona fide hero of mine, who served in our embassy in Stockholm, directed me to spot, develop and recruit agents primarily among anti-communist exiles from the Baltic republics that were being incorporated into the growing Soviet empire.

In preparation for WWIII, I drew maps of potential drop and landing zones for use by stay-behind nets in the event of a Soviet occupation of Sweden. (One fellow in central Sweden may still have two thousand liters of gasoline stored under his barn for use by our stay-behind agents.) This sounds a lot like fun and games today, but it was serious business in the early days of CIA when covert operations were divided into two compartmented units–one for intelligence collection and one for propaganda and political action operations. Included in the latter component was the creation of stay-behind nets to be activated in the event of a third world war.

Colby provided me with on-the-job training in how to develop my own non-official cover employment as a free-lance broadcaster and writer. He also used me for various secret missions that required the hand of the U.S. government to be concealed. One such assignment involved my delivery of a brief case of Polish currency to a member of the Polish resistance organization, an old woman who lived in a one-room hovel in the university town of Lund in southern Sweden. I recall how this woman insisted that I have a cup of coffee with her before getting down to business. Then she counted the currency out loud in Polish, which made it sound like she was whistling a folk song. She then signed a receipt and I departed until my next delivery of funds for use by Polish patriots fighting against their Soviet oppressors in the Cold War. This activity and my secret work with Estonian and Latvian refugee students at the University of Stockholm where I had studied under the G.I. Bill in 1974-1948 constituted my Cold War baptism of fire. It became personal. The Baltic republics, which were created after WW I, had become early victims of Soviet imperialism. They were – and still are – among the most wonderful people in the world. I will never forget how these little kids sang "Jingle Bells" at a Christmas party we American students at the University of Stockholm gave for them in 1948.

Of course, Bill Colby, who firmly believed in on-the-job training of deep-cover staff agents like me saw to it that I was kept busy with a variety of assignments that would enhance my experience and keep me busy (and excited) with work on the street. He created one such *ad hoc* assignment from a small item in the local press, which reported that a visiting delegation from Red China had been evicted from their fleabag hotel because of preparing Chinese stir- fry cuisine in their room. Bill sent a message to me through his secretary (we met for these meetings in secluded out of the way locations in Stockhom) to visit the hotel, get the names of the Chinese Communist visitors and any details of their undiplomatic behavior. I did so and my story was picked up by several European newspapers to the embarrassment of Mao's recently installed communist government in Peking. Mission accomplished.

Before leaving the subject of non-official cover, I should mention that there are certain risks and problems involved in the arrangement. One is the risk that the cover job might become more attractive both financially and in terms of job satisfaction than working secretly part-time (at all hours of the night and day) for the government. To reduce this problem, non-official (NOC) cover has been made a career service option, with special incentives to employees who are willing and able to make a commitment to this particularly demanding career path.

Another risk is that an officer assigned abroad under a non-official cover arrangement, sometimes with little more than an answering service as a business telephone number, may have his cover effectively destroyed through no fault of his own. I knew of one case where an officer with thin commercial cover became the victim of whispered gossip that he was a secret CIA agent spread in the local business club by a fellow American business competitor.

Personally, I loved almost every minute of the special challenges and satisfactions offered by a NOC career, and I'm still benefiting from the Agency's retirement benefits. At the same time, I understand and respect all the young men and women officers who work in the CIA who may be ill-suited to handle the special stress that goes with living under non-official cover, living with – sometimes sleeping with – your briefcase.

In my case, it was a former vice-president of CBS News, Sig Mickelsen, who shortly after I retired sought to settle a career grievance with his former boss by blowing the whistle on my use of journalist cover. His disclosure, though it was denied by executives named by him, nevertheless effectively caused me to be professionally blacklisted. The doors to my employment in the field of journalism were permanently closed. Like victims of the Sen. McCarthy witch hunts in the 1950's, I was effectively blacklisted, prevented from working as a journalist/broadcaster, the only career for which I was qualified.

D Is For Delbert

His name was Delbert (not Dilbert) Vastbinder, and with a name like that you just knew that this boy would one day end up in prison or as the president of an Ivy League college. Turned out that he ended up in jail after several detours from the path of conventional behavior initiated at the elementary school level in my home town of Battle Creek, Michigan. In brief, Delbert seems to have had trouble coming up with an acceptable excuse for his unauthorized acquisition of other people's property. His entire life was based on a sort of spontaneous moral code that made right any action he might take to satisfy a momentary desire. For example, in fourth grade Delbert took my sled home with him from school. Why? According to his beautiful mother's explanation, he took the sled because it was such fun riding it down the hill alongside Fremont Elementary school. Did he intend to return it to its rightful owner? Why, of course he did. He wouldn't *steal* it, she said. And I'm sure, in retrospect, that Delbert never considered what he helped himself to as theft. He simply borrowed things from other people that he needed or wanted. After WW II, Delbert was arrested and incarcerated for breaking into Goode's Bakery in the wee hours of the morning to take some delicacies from the store show case. His explanation - not an alibi - was as brief as it was truthful: "I was hungry."

It would be unfair to leave the impression that Delbert was in some way assigned to a social cubby hole outside the mainstream of his generation. He was just one of the guys – most of the time. Now and then, however, Delbert's sense of humor put him in a special place. There was the day, for example, when our 5th grade teacher, the Chinese-American Miss Loy, made five or six of us remain in our seats after school until the miscreant in our midst confessed to a certain anti-social behavior he had engaged in that had made us all laugh. Five or ten minutes passed in silence, which was only broken when Delbert shifted in his seat ever so slightly to make room for a gaseous emission to be rattled off the seat on which he was seated. Miss Loy, slowly stood up, put down the textbook she had in her hands, turned her shaking back to her class and quietly intoned "class dismissed."

Another boy who couldn't seem to avoid ending up on the wrong side of approved social behavior was Carl Geyer, the son of a onetime

Battle Creek, Michigan, school superintendent and kid brother of a boy who was so straight in his behavior that he was nicknamed *Arrow*. Carl had such a winning personality that even when neighbors became aware of his anti-social habits, they just couldn't help liking him. So everyone hoped that service in the U.S. Navy would finally put Carl on the straight and narrow. Unfortunately that was a road that Carl avoided like the plague. Even at the end of WWII, when all Carl had to do was report back to his duty station at the Great Lakes Naval Training Station in Chicago after a 12-hour liberty, he disappeared from sight until found by the Navy shore patrol and sent to the brig. His discharge was *less than honorable*, as was his postwar career on the edge of or across the border of criminal activity.

D is for Dogs

In India it is said that a man can be truly judged by his regard for and treatment of animals. The reason for this is simply that animals cannot in any tangible way repay the kindness bestowed upon them by their owners. In my own experience this certainly proved to be true.. The four for whom I served as nominal master over the past half century enriched my life above and beyond measure and received in return nothing more than a warm bed, lots of exercise, fresh air, food, water and an occasional adventure

Binker

My first puppy arrived as a surprise present from my parents when I was twelve and he was just eight-weeks old. He was a little black cocker spaniel with long ears and a wavy coal-black coat. There was no problem giving him a name, since Binker arrived as the incarnation of the little rascal of that name created by the English poet A.A. Milne who had long romped about on the pages of my favorite bedtime story. My parents made me responsible for taking care of Binker, which included feeding him table scraps and an occasional handful of kibbles, and cleaning up after him. A wooden box lined with an old towel was provided for my dog to use as his bed. This rule was strictly enforced by Binker's master for an hour, at which time I decided that it was my duty to bring him into my bed to prevent his crying from disturbing the sleep of my parents in their bedroom next to mine.

Captain

The next time a dog entered my life was after the war, after college, after I got married and after I moved to Stockholm on my first overseas assignment with the Central Intelligence Agency. This puppy was, like Binker, a pedigreed black cocker spaniel. He was ordered by mail. My late wife Vesla and I picked him up at *Centralen* railroad station in Stockholm on a cold winter evening in December, 1952. We had no children at the time and so Captain became our first baby. We were living in a proletarian single bedroom apartment complex on the south side of Stockholm a 20-miute drive from downtown in my 1946 Ford two-door sedan.

My first memorable experience with Captain took place on the dozen wooden steps that descended from our street, Vikstensvaegan, down to the ground-level gravel path that wound its way through the woods to the shopping center. One day as I started down the steps with Captain we encountered a young boy with tousled blonde hair about half way up the stairs. He stopped, took off his cap, and politely asked "Kan farbror lyfta den der hunden upp i luften?" (Can uncle lift that dog up in the air?) I immediately answered this challenge to my strength by lifting Captain up to chest level, whereupon the young boy passed by and walked up a few steps before turning around. He tipped his cap and with a big smile on his face said "Takk saa mycket." (Thank you very much) before proceeding up the steps. And I was left silently holding my dog in the air, too embarrassed to say "vaer saa god" ("you're welcome")

A few weeks later Captain embarrassed me again. We had invited a couple to dinner and were having a drink when suddenly I heard my wife scream from the kitchen. There stood our puppy dog licking his chops as the last of four filet mignon steaks that were to be served for dinner disappeared down his gullet. We had to take the couple to dinner at a downtown restaurant priced far beyond our means. I could have killed that animal. Instead, Captain spent most of his life being spoiled rotten by Vesla's family in Oslo, Norway.

Suzy

In Voorburg a suburb of The Hague, capital of the Netherlands, Vesla and I adopted a mixed breed shepherd puppy we named Suzy. She was a wonderful dog and a faithful companion of our first son, Austin Jay. But occasionally this was a mixed blessing. One day I got a call at my office from my clearly distraught wife, who said I had to come home at once. It turned out that Jay had led Suzy out onto the railway bridge over the Vliet canal behind out house, and the station master had managed to get the boy and dog off the bridge only seconds before the Amsterdam-Rotterdam express train passed through.

At the same residence, Austin Jay decided on a hot summer to cool off with Suzy in the little feeder canal behind our house. In they went, with our top-heavy maid Cobie in hot pursuit to prevent a double drowning in the canal water. Instead the canal nearly flooded its banks as Cobie dove in to rescue the itinerant boy and dog in the nick of time.

Bamsa

This cream-colored puppy of mixed parentage joined our family when we set out to build our log home constructed of pre-cut fir timbers that were shipped from Norway to the rolling hills of Fairfax County just down the road from the River Bend Golf and Country Club in Great Falls, Virginia in the early seventies. Vesla had fallen in love with the five-acre wooded lot which featured a creek that wound along its western boundary and we bought it before we left for our tour of duty in Frankfurt Germany in 1970. Bamsa claimed seniority on the property, which gave him the right to enforce a speed limit of 3 mph on our 250-yard roadway leading north off Beach Mill Rd.

Bamsa had cleared a shortcut under the weeds from our house to our private road that enabled him to intercept – and if necessary slow down - any car leaving our house en route to Beach Mill Road. It once took our good friend Marilyn Dale 20 minutes to cover the 250 yards out to the main road.

Lobo

This pup, who resembled Bamsa, was acquired in Bangkok where he served as the protector of our fenced house off Soi Sukhumvit (#64). When we returned to the U.S., Lobo remained behind to live with our servants, my chauffuer/gardener Prayoo and his wife, Somsi, our cook/maid. Earlier, in an apartment off Soi 64, we had a little black and white mutt who was run over by a car outside our house. Workers in the area laughed as we buried him, and I had to explain to my angry sons that this was not a sign of disrespect but of grief by the animal-loving Thai construction workers.

Darby

Darby was a black Lab of mixed parentage who resided at and governed St. Augustine Road in Hubertus, Wisconsin. This gently rolling land in the Kettle Morrane district a half an hour's drive north of Milwaukee is the birthplace of Mona, who had already acquired Darby when she and Austin got together. He liked Austin, whom he immediately sized up as a dog lover, but he pretty much stuck by his life style, which involved patrolling the area that covered several square miles. In the evening, it took Darby at least five minutes to get past Austin's book and onto his lap. For his strenuous patrol work, Darby required and got two large daily helpings of food, including a hand-out from neighbors who loved him as much as we did. They are now Darby's beloved and loving owners.

Arrow (for his speed) and *Monty* (for Montgomery) are the current protectors of the home in Port Washington, Wisconsin, which they graciously share with Mona and Austin and their beloved daughter Sammy, who's away most of the time in college at the University of Wisconsin- Milwaukee. These Mutt and Jeff boys are both protective and cuddling housemates and watch dogs. Finally, loving mention should be made of our grey tiger kitty, Jason, who mostly hangs out in and around Sammy's bedroom in the lower level of our home where she occasionally wards off visits by her canine buddies from upstairs with a lion's snarl.

E Is For Espionage

When we collect information on the plans and capabilities of other nations without their consent (or often even their knowledge) it's called espionage. The activity is creative and often exciting. As a kid, I recall the secret pleasure of stealing a penny or two (never more) from the little drawer in the upper middle section of Mother's desk, which had a key in place on the outside but was never locked. I came to suspect that Mother planted those pennies deliberately to test the honesty of her children. Once, in the course of examining the contents of the drawer I discovered a nickel. Now, really, how could my mother think I was stupid enough to incriminate myself by stealing a whole nickel?

Hiding places were an important aspect of my childhood indoctrination in the fine arts of secret intelligence work for which my childhood prepared me and may have propelled me. The floor boards in the attic at 38 Elizabeth Street were perfectly suited to the secret storage of personal goods. When I first painstakingly sawed a board width of flooring to create a place to cache my booty, I failed to note that the work left a tell-tale scar. This had to be covered with a scrap of old carpeting cut from a remote corner of the attic rug. And I was made aware of a major pitfall in all clandestine activity: It is easy, in fact inevitable, to leave visible tracks of such action but difficult to cover them from unwanted observation. I found this out a few years later when I had to cover the marks left behind where I buried a secret radio set in the winter forests of Finland for use by stay-behind nets to be activated in the event of a Soviet occupation in World War III. But when the snow melted, the ground sank to reveal the outline of the cache, which had to be repaired when I fortunately returned to check out the site several months later.

In preparing a stay-behind network for activation in WW III, my boss was Bill Colby, who had served with the OSS in the second world war, when he was parachuted into occupied France and Germany to work with resistance groups. This bona fide hero of mine, who served in our embassy in Stockholm directed me to recruit and train stay-behind agents to set up secret resistance groups and to plant secret caches of weapons and other materials This sounds like fun a lot of and games today, but it was serious business in the early days of CIA when covert operations were divided into two compartmented units—one for intelligence collection and one for propaganda and political action operations, including the creation of stay-behind nets to be activated in a third world war.

Bill Colby encouraged me to diversify my cover activities to provide maximum flexibility to cover my absences from home on Agency assignments that had to be kept out of the public eye. I called this lateral diversification, and it worked like this: If I normally would have attended a press conference but had a meeting scheduled with a secret agent at the same time, I'd have to have a fall back excuse for my absence. Beyond illness or a normally confidential meeting with a member of the opposite sex, neither of which should be overused, I could explain that I had to meet a businessman who needed help in getting a speech translated into English, or I had to complete a rush translation of a sales presentation, or whatever. The main idea was to have at the ready an excuse to explain my location at any given time or place. This multi-faceted, flexible form of cover employment served me well for a score of years working as a deep-cover secret CIA agent overseas.

Of course, as with every aspect of life in the world of secret operations, luck plays a huge role. One officer who came to Stockholm with a neatly designed and documented commercial cover was identified as a secret CIA agent by another American businessman in a whispered revelation to members of the local businessmen's club. He had no evidence to support this disabling assertion, but none was needed. He simply used the medium of gossip to undermine the credentials of a business competitor. The damage was done to the viability of the agent's cover and he returned to a Headquarters job in Washington after a brief tour of duty abroad.

There were, of course, several secret assignments that needed to be carried out for which there could be no plausible cover story. One such job involved the transportation of a large briefcase of Polish currency to a member of the Polish resistance, who lived in a two-room hovel in the university town of Lund several hours train ride south of Stockholm. It was impossible for me to insult this lady and her lonely service to her homeland by simply shoving the currency under her doormat. First of all it would be rude. This nice old lady always insisted that I have a coup of coffee with her before our transaction. Apart from a few words of Swedish we had no common language, so after sharing our coffee mostly in smiling silence we got down to business. She counted the currency out loud in Polish, which made it sound like she was whistling a sprightly tune. Then she signed a receipt and I departed until my next delivery of funds for use by Polish patriots fighting against their Soviet oppressors in the Cold War. This activity and my secret work with Estonian and Latvian refugee students at the University of Stockholm where I had studied under the G.I. Bill in 1974-1948 constituted my Cold War baptism of fire.

Bill Colby, who firmly believed in on-the-job training of deep-cover staff agents like me, saw to it that I was kept busy with a variety of assignments that would enhance my experience and keep me busy (and excited) with work on the street. He created one *ad hoc* assignment from a small item in the local press that reported how a visiting delegation from Red China had been evicted from their fleabag downtown hotel because they prepared Chinese stir fry cuisine in their room. Bill sent a message to me through his secretary (we met for these meetings in secluded out of the way locations) to visit the hotel, get the names of the Chinese Communist visitors and any details of their undiplomatic behavior. Then get it published. I did so and my story was picked up by several European newspapers to the embarrassment of Mao's recently installed communist government in Peking. Mission accomplished.

Before leaving the subject of non-official cover, I should mention that there are certain risks involved in the arrangement. One is the risk that the cover job might become more attractive both financially and in terms of job satisfaction than working secretly part-time (at all hours of the night and day) for the CIA. To reduce this problem, non-official (NOC) cover has been made a career service option, with special incentives to employees who are willing and able to make the commitment to this career path.

Personally, I loved almost every minute of the special challenges and satisfactions offered by a NOC career in the CIA. At the same time, I understand and respect all the young men and women officers employed in the CIA who may be ill-suited to handle the special stress that goes with living under non-official cover.

E is for Etz

Normally I have trouble remembering birthdays, but I always remember that my kid sister Ethel Adele Goodrich, who somehow got the nickname "Etz," was born on Armistice Day, November 11th. I was already eight years old at the time and I suppose resented her arrival to replace me as the family *baby*.

Of her early childhood I only recall the profound grief we all shared when she became sick and had to be taken to Leila Hospital to be treated for a strep infection that was often fatal in the days before antibiotics. It was the first time I can remember doing some serious praying, closed in my bedroom closet on my knees next to a wicker basket full of dirty laundry. My Dad found me there. Startled by his presence, I started to rise but he put his hand on my shoulder and assured me that God hears our prayers at any time or place, that it matters not where or when we call on Him for help. Well, God heard and Etz came back home to occupy the bedroom that had been renovated from a screened porch at the back of our childhood home at 38 Elizabeth Street.

In retrospect, I'm struck by the sharp line of age demarcation struck by World War II. Those of us who got into our teens before the war were carefree, okay, wild. We drove cars as soon as we were able to get a license when we were 14 years old, went on dates in dance halls, drank gallons of beer (laced with bourbon when it was available) and generally behaved as more or less untamed kids . Ethel and her peers born in the late Depression years but before World War II moved through their teens almost soundlessly.

Or at least it seemed like that to me.

Etz went to college at Oberlin College, where she met and later married her sweetheart, Garry Ackerson, who tragically was killed in an auto accident a few blocks from their home after he had served as a jet fighter pilot in the Marine Air Force. The couple lived in Grand Rapids, MI, and before that in Toronto, Canada. Their three wonderful children who live in Maine and Colorado get together as a family every August at Crystal Lake, in northern Michigan. The tradition of summer holidays at this lake goes back to the 30's when the Goodrich family always spent a week there in a white fame cottage owned by Uncle Bill, who owned a furniture store in Owosso MI..

F Is for Fun and Games

Work abroad as a career staff agent in the Central Intelligence Agency was not always a stressful job devoid of comic relief. Occasionally we'd get a chuckle or two out of serving in the world's second oldest profession. Our adversaries clearly enjoyed the advantage of immunity from hostile scrutiny by their media or legislative committees. But we had the advantage of being able to pull their humorless chains.

On one occasion, I turned one of their historical celebrations into a propaganda victory for our side and an embarrassment for theirs. My unwitting launching pad for the operation was a small communist weekly newspaper which had recently announced the 25th anniversary of its founding in hopes of generating financial donations. (For some reason, perhaps because of their fixation with the Marxist theory of historical necessity, communist media have a thing about celebrating anniversaries for fund raising.)

So one night I dusted off my old Halda typewriter and wrote:

"Comrades! Congratulations on your 25th anniversary! Your fraternal allies salute your excellent work in the service of proletarian internationalism! We look forward to the time when Finland will be able to become a full partner in the family of people's democracies.
Yuri A. Karpov
First Secretary of the Soviet Embassy"

The ostensible writer of the message was a ranking member of the Soviet KGB mission at the local Soviet Embassy who had been identified to us by a KGB defector as an unusually competent officer regarded as a rising star in the Soviet intelligence service.

I scribbled Karpov's signature and slipped the letter into a plain envelope along with a local currency note worth about three US dollars. I then affixed postage on the envelope and dropped it in a mail box down the street from the Soviet Embassy – just two blocks from my apartment overlooking Helsinki harbor – in the moonlight. A few days later I was surprised to see my letter printed in the newspaper along with several other congratulatory messages. It was published exactly as written except for one detail: the published version had corrected a small grammatical error in my text.

Then the fit hit the shan, so to speak. Helsingin Sanomat, the leading Finnish daily, screamed in editorial outrage about the Soviet diplomatic mission for authoring a message that blatantly disrespected Finland's neutrality. News media in Helsinki and in the provinces joined in the outrage over the Soviet letter. A few days later the Soviet embassy denounced the letter as a forgery, but this denial of authorship and the tabloid's red-faced retraction did little to diminish the popular outrage over its message.

In fact, the Soviet denials of responsibility for the letter produced a backlash among their Finnish comrades in at least one case. A writer of a letter to the editor of a provincial communist newspaper wondered in print what the fuss was all about. He wrote: "Isn't Finland's membership in the family of peoples democracies what we want for our country?" In the next general elections the Finnish electorate answered this question with a resounding defeat of Communist Party candidates.

Karpov was recalled to Moscow "for medical reasons" several months short of his assigned tour of duty, and so far as I know he never got another assignment outside the USSR. I sincerely hope that he suffered no further damage to his career from a KGB investigation that probably lasted for several months.

As for the poor night editor of the Finnish Communist tabloid I can only say: "Thanks for correcting the grammatical mistake in my letter, and I hope you found gainful employment in another, less politically sensitive, line of work."

Footnote: This article was previously published in BORN TO SPY, Recollections of a CIA Officer, by Austin Goodrich, iUniverse, 2004.

G is for Gutekunst, Dad's Name

I'm glad that my Father, Cyrus John Goodrich, Attorney at Law, changed our family name to Goodrich before I was born even though there are a number of persons bearing our original family name of Gutekunst who have produced fine careers in many fields. I suspect that my mother, who used to teach the German language and loved everything about the history and culture of her husband's ancestors regretted the name change. In any case, I was always glad that I wasn't saddled with a name that could be used to create a number of obscene nicknames. (I'll leave it to the reader to imagine some of them.)

The only time that I ever heard my father use a German word was on the very rare occasions when he lost his temper and screamed a curse in that tongue. The German for "Fear the Devil" was one phrase that occasionally shook the rafters at 38 Elizabeth Street, but I could count on the fingers of one hand the number of times he shouted it, usually to vent displeasure with some stupid action of his children. Like when I threw I threw a pillow at my sister that flew over her head and hit a candle stick on the dining room buffet which cracked a piece of my mother's favorite china bowl standing behind it.

I recall that my dad's father, my grandpa with a red moustache, who had moved the family from a farm in Hickory Corners into Marshall, the Calhoun County seat, knew very little English, but refused to speak German.. I can only recall hearing non-verbal loving sounds crossing his lips. How he managed to raise a family of eight kids without using the language that they learned in school I do not know. I have to believe that he knew his family's native tongue but simply refused to use it. One possible explanation may have been that he and my grandmother came from different parts of Germany and used English (limited as it was) as the best mans of hurdling the communications barrier of two different German dialects. My mother, who occasionally taught German, thought this to be the case. Anyway, I was impressed and delighted to hear my father, who had a great tenor voice, sing *Die Lorelei* in German when the song was played over the boat's loudspeakers on our Rhine River cruise in 1962. It was on that happy sojourn that my octogenarian Dad showed me up big time by climbing to the top of the tall Strasbourg Cathedral, leaving me panting two floors behind.

My Dad, known by his close friends as "Cy," a nickname I happily accepted, loved sports. He coached baseball in the high school where he taught in the Upper Peninsula before entering law school at his (and my) beloved University of Michigan. We used to play catch, but he realized early on that I lacked the coordination required to excel in that sport. This was brought home rather dramatically once when he tossed a baseball to me on our porch steps. My reaction was so slow that the missile sailed between my hands and conked me on the head. After that he fully supported my sport (football) and attended all my high school games, which were boycotted by my mother who hated the game and the cuts and bruises it often sent me home with.

I can say with absolute certainty that my mother never set foot in the great University of Michigan football Stadium known as "The Big House" in Ann Arbor, where my Dad and I have personalized bricks at the main (southwestern) entrance gate. Mine is inscribed with *Ne'er Forget*, his with *Hail to the Victors*. Mother did, however, accompany Dad and me to the parking lot where she claims to have listened to the game on the car radio. I doubt this. More likely she listened to a symphony orchestra concert beamed to Ann Arbor all the way from New York City's Rockefeller Center.

I shall forever honor and cherish the memory of my father, Cyrus John Goodrich, son of a farmer/carpenter, who had to teach school in Michigan's Upper Peninsula for several years to raise funds to pay for his professional education at the University of Michigan Law School in Ann Arbor. While he built a successful law practice in Battle Creek, Michigan, he devoted most of his professional time in his later years to represent financially-strapped clients who had been victimized by unscrupulous loan sharks and finance companies. At the time of my father's death, a Michigan judge told my mother that Dad fought for these destitute workers and farmers with the zeal and tenacity of an attorney half his age. My father was and forever will remain enshrined in my memory as the best role model a kid ever had.

H is For Helen

I suppose that all humanoids inhabiting our planet reserve a special place in their memories for a few special people and places. Don't get me wrong. Picking a particular person and place in no way suggests any kind of evaluative ranking of objects loved. It's just that certain persons, places and events stand out in an especially memorable way in the kaleidoscope of my rear vision mirror. The letter H evokes the indelible appearance in my mind's eye of a person, my big sister Helen and a city, Helsinki, capital of Finland.

Helen Goodrich will long be remembered in the annals of Battle Creek Central High School, home of the Bearcats, as one of two outstanding beauties in the class of 1937. The other was Mary Lou Gordon. All the others were just teenage high school girls.

During her high school days, Helen was courted, as could be expected by a virtual caravan of boys. There was Bob Morse, a big, handsome Bearcat football tackle and a role model of mine; "Fig" Newton who had a cottage on Gull Lake; Bob Beach, who lived just down the street, and a score of others seeking Helen's favor. Now, Helen did not want to play favorites, she wanted to play the field, and by golly, that's what she did. It wasn't merely a numbers game. It was that my big sister dreaded the possibility, remote as it was, of being without a date to take her out on a weekend evening. This all too often (certainly in the perception of my parents) led to there being more than one boy in quest of Helen's company seated in our living room on weekend evenings. Sometimes Helen dispatched me, her kid brother, to sneak downstairs, scout the field and report back to her the names (or descriptions if I didn't know their names) of her suitors nervously awaiting her appearance.

I can't recall how Helen managed to thin down her tribe of admirers, but I do recall that her daddy and I were often left to play critical roles in the charade.

When sister Nonne - halfway between Hellie and me in age - started to seriously date a couple of years later we often had a packed parlor situation that challenged the diplomatic skills of our attorney father. Fortunately, Jack "Lunnie" Langs avoided the living room in favor of cruising back and forth in front of our house in his parents' 1932 Buick coupe seeking to draw Nonne's -and only Nonne's - attention outside. (It should be mentioned that this car's slow idle speed enabled the driver to leave it in gear, get out and walk alongside it an entire block at a leisurely pace if it took that long to attract a certain person's attention. Try that little trick today and I'll guarantee you that the car you're driving will either stall out or run into the nearest fire hydrant, leaving its driver spilled in the gutter.)

After high school, Hellie left to attend Stephens College in Springfield, MO, the first of us to go off to college in our parents' footsteps. (Dad had graduated from rhe University of Michigan Law School '13 and Mom had graduated from little Wells College in upstate New York.) Sister Eleanor and I both managed to get through the University of Michigan within a year of each other in the late 40's, and baby sister Ethel graduated from Oberlin College, a private college in Oberlin, Ohio, several years later. There "Etz" met and later married her college sweetheart, Garret, "Gary" Ackerson.

It was during the war that Helen met, fell in love with, became engaged to and married Lieutenant Vincent C. "Vince" Guerin in the Army chapel at Fort Custer, located a dozen miles outside Battle Creek. The happy couple had announced their engagement in a dramatic if somewhat unconventional (not to mention inconvenient) manner. It happened some time around midnight when they barged up the stairs (there was no other way to climb those creaky stairs), burst into our parents' bedroom and shouted their joyful news: "We're going to get married!"

Well, it was a beautiful occasion for a traditional military wedding (crossed sabers and all) at the little white New England style chapel on the post, home of the Army's 5th Infantry Division. Before Vince was transferred to an anti-tank battalion at a camp in Texas (and deployment to combat in the European Theatre) the couple enjoyed an extended honeymoon in a cottage they rented from one of Hellie's high school beaus, Bill "Fig" Newton, on Gull Lake. Thanks to the couple's gracious hospitality, some of my high school buddies and I enjoyed a beer 'n pretzels bash in their cottage on more than one occasion.

Fast forward to '44 when I managed to sneak out of Camp Benning outside Columbus, GA, to meet Hellie and Vince for an overnight in Atlanta. We had dinner together at a grand hotel ballroom where I felt like the only enlisted man in the room. How embarrassing! Anyway, before returning to camp the next morning, I asked Vince to scribble a brief note to explain that I had been with him and my sister for an overnight visit. Vince did so, although somewhat reluctantly, I thought. I later realized that he ran a serious risk of loosing his commission for this action, since I was actually AWOL at the time. Anyway, thank God, my misdeed went unnoticed and I didn't cost my wonderful brother-in-arms his commission!

When the war ended, Vince dutifully took his honorable discharge and embarked on a civilian career in the business world. The couple first rented an apartment in Illinois where I visited them briefly on my way home from the Army. I recall how out of place Vince looked in a civilian suit of clothes. When he put on a snap-brim hat it just didn't seem to fit right however he placed it. Clearly, his head was not designed for a civilian lid. After training briefly with U.S. Steel, Helen and Vince returned to the place where they were meant to be: the United States Army.

If Vince was born to be an Army officer, Helen was just as surely meant to be an Army officer's wife. She moved gracefully in and out of a dozen permanent changes of address, including posts in Germany and Japan, while serving as wife and mother of three fine children: Eleanor (aka Elly), Jeanne Ellen and Vincent Austin. Some years after Vince's untimely death from cancer, Hellie retained her position as an honored member of the Army family by marrying retired Army General George Putnam.

H is for Helsinki

Helsinki, Finland, is very simply the best kept secret in Western Europe. Those of us who know this to be true are tacitly pledged to keep the fact secret. lest the capital of Finland become inundated with tourists and lose its special character. When I lived there (1958-1960) Helsinki just barely qualified as a metropolis with a population of 400,000 souls. It was located on a harbor filled with boats, the most attractive women in the world and a tree-lined green park with space for a band in the summer and an ice rink in the winter. The main street named after a national hero (Carl Gustaf Mannerheim) provided easy access by foot or street car to all major points of interest, including hotels, the stadium (site of 1952 Olympics), parliament, the presidential residence, theatre, opera house, department stores, cinemas and offices buildings. No small wonder that Helsinki became acclaimed as an early model of efficient urban planning. It remains a strikingly beautiful harbor city on the Gulf of Finland.

On my first visit to this Venice of the North (a title shared with Stockholm) in 1948, Helsinki stood at an east-west political crossroads. In January, Czechoslovakia had voted the Soviet-backed Communist Party into power and it appeared that the communist-led left wing party (the SKDL) might bring Finland into the Soviet orbit along the same path. When my sister Eleanor and I visited, Helsinki was the scene of huge market place demonstrations in support of the communist bloc candidates led by the spell-binding orator Hertta Kuusinen, daughter of a ranking member of the ruling communist party of the Soviet Union, O.V. Kuusinen. It was a tense and scary scene that we'll never forget.

Some days later in Frankfurt, West Germany we experienced at first hand the miracle pulled off by economic wizard Ludvig Erhardt, who turned the dormant economy around on an historic Sunday by issuing new currency and ending rationing.

Later we experienced a dangerous east-west confrontation in Italy where the communist party challenged for power and we were briefly caught up in a communist-led general strike that nearly paralyzed the country and stranded us in the Communist stronghold of Arezzo, Tuscany, for two days. When we tried to get to Rome by taxi, we were turned back by a Communist squad armed with submachine guns. It would be no exaggeration to say that Nonne and I witnessed at first-hand an historical turning point when east and west avoided WW III by settling into a prolonged but bloodless cold war.

One of my assignments during nearly three years in Helsinki was to drive out into the countryside in the dark of night to bury waterproof-sealed radio sets and signal plans for eventual use by stay-behind secret agents in case of war with the Soviet Union. In the NATO countries of Western Europe this secret work was carried out jointly with the intelligence services of these countries. In Finland we had to do the job of developing these secret networks on our own. That gave me a special sense of pride in my work.

My first residence in Helsinki was located on a granite outcropping in a park *Brunnsparken)* overlooking the harbor and two small islands which housed the Yacht Club and a Night Club respectively. In the summer months, these sites could be reached by a small ferry boat. In the winter, residents of the islands and people who worked there could walk across ice when it was thick enough to support their weight. Needless to say, this involved a potentially perilous judgment call.

While the overnight Stockholm-Helsinki ferry was operating, these ships tied up directly in front of my apartment building, which I shall always remember as the best place in the world to live, the frigid winter months notwithstanding. When sister Nonne and I crossed the Baltic, we and hundreds of other passengers unable to afford staterooms slept on deck or in the ship's corridors. Somehow it was possible, even enjoyable, to survive with practically no sleep during the months illuminated by the midnight sun. Some years later I accompanied a group of foreign correspondents on a five-day tour north of the Arctic Circle. As the honored guests of five Arctic cities, we were wined and dined into the wee hours of the morning, and never suffered any ill effects, not a single hangover. I'll never know why this was. The Scandinavians simply call it *Lappsjuka* (Lapp disease), and it may explain why people who live at the northern latitudes find it difficult to live anywhere else.

Next door to my wonderful harbor-side residence in Helsinki stands a modest gray frame house once occupied by Carl Gustaf Mannerheim, leader of Finland's wars against the Soviet Red Army in the early 1940's. The residence now serves as a museum to commemorate the life of the man who led Finland during its David vs Goliath wars to preserve its independence of its powerful next door neighbor, the Soviet Union.

One price paid by Finland for losing its second WW II war with the USSR was having to lease to the Soviet Union a naval base at Porkkala on the Gulf of Finland just west of Helsinki. When my sister and I took the train from Turku on the Baltic Sea to Helsinki, our railway car was literally shuttered with corrugated steel curtains as we passed through the base. This was a security measure presumably designed to prevent Finnish passengers from spying on the Soviet installation. We recall to this day how Finnish passengers sat silently looking straight ahead during the hour delay on the trip. After the Soviet lease expired and the Soviets returned the base, Finnish authorities had to demolish the Soviet buildings which were deemed uninhabitable for reasons of public health.

Before leaving Helsinki, I have to return for a retro look at the Western Foreign Press Club, which had been organized and was led by Lancelot Allan Keyworth, Finnish correspondent of the Financial Times of London and Time-Life magazine. Lance was married to the widowed wife of a Finnish 5,000 meter Olympics champion who had been killed in the Winter War with the USSR. In addition to our Saturday luncheon meetings, we were occasionally invited by Finnish corporations seeking publicity in the west to tour their companies and share their hospitality at luncheons that often staggered quite literally into the late evening hours. Once a dozen of us cooled down after being parboiled in the company *sauna* baths by jumping through holes chopped in the ice in lakes outside their corporate offices.

I recall how we held our Saturday meetings in the press room at the Kemp Hotel. When this fell on May 1st, it was an honored Press Club tradition to stand on the 2nd floor balcony there and raise our glasses to the trade unionists marching below in the May Day parade. The marchers were not amused and returned our salute with clenched fists. Fortunately Scandinavian workers gained economic and political power, including equal representation on corporate boards, without having to resort to armed struggle.

H is for Hitchhiking

Websters: *To travel by asking for rides from motorists along the way*

It's sort of like life itself, isn't it? I mean no one's moving along all alone. Regardless of where we're heading on this unmarked path, half the time we don't even know where we're going or what we're going to do when we get there. But it's comforting to know that we're not alone. A hitchhiker is never alone, except between rides. Maybe that's why we liked, needed, to hitchhike. But now – like so many other good things in our society – it's over. Gone and done with. Ended mainly by the insurance companies. You know, the folks who guarantee us a soft landing wherever we go, whatever stupid thing we might do. But I don't care. I still want to bum a ride even if I have to dig back in my memory to get one.

It must have been in the summer of 1940 the between year when the Depression would finally end and the War would get started. For us, that is. Oh, those countries on the other side of the ocean were fighting, but that didn't really matter. They were always fighting. What mattered was the need we felt to get in a few days of vacation before going back to school. I had spent most of the summer working at a machine shop to earn money ($7.50 per week) and to build up strength for football. At least that's how my Dad put a gentle spin on what he saw as the need to get me off the street and out of jail where a game of craps played in a storefront had landed me a few months earlier. "Happy" Harpster, who had been similarly encouraged by *his* father to find gainful (and legal) employment also needed to get in some vacation time. As did young Jim Buchanan, who never got into any trouble but enjoyed the company of those who did.

Destination: Ludington, Michigan on the lake of the same name. There were beaches much closer to our hometown of Battle Creek, but they were all touristy places without well-paying jobs. Jim and I had secretly decided to encourage our 16-year-old partner Happy to get a well-paying job in a factory. We were too young. Yes, on the kind of money that Dow Chemical paid, we would be able to live like kings! Trouble is, Happy was never a party to the plan, and his aversion to manual labor proved too much for our scheme to oversome.

Nevertheless, posing as teenage innocents dressed like Boy Scout campers, knapsacks and all, we made it to Ludington, mostly as talkative guests of sleepy truck drivers. Unfortunately, local hotels refused to accept our allegiance to God and country in lieu of cold hard cash, and we set up camp on, where else, the beach. Now it seems impossible that the temperature could drop from ninety degrees at noon to below freezing at midnight, but I swear that's what it did. So after two more days of fruitless attempts to get Happy into a job, and devoid of cash, we decided to end our vacation and head home.

We somehow got to Kalamazoo, 25 miles from home base at an intersection with a traffic light. People turning right had to be driving to Battle Creek, there being no other choice. Nevertheless, drivers took a long look at us, locked their doors and sped on without us. After a couple of hours, we decided to split up. Jim wisely volunteered to go it alone, and he was promptly picked up. Another two hours passed and no Samaritan appeared to give us a lift. One look at Happy explained our problem. With a scruffy black beard, he was the image of a mean and possibly dangerous man. And we both smelt bad. With the prospect looming of having to spend the night on that intersection, Happy and I exchanged a look that said "let's go for it." They were a kindly old couple that smiled as we piled into the back seat of their Chevy a second before they could lock the doors. So we got home, having learned that personal appearance may not be everything, but it's important when seeking rides from strangers.

After the war I got back into hitchhiking to get from college in Ann Arbor to Battle Creek where my family and my girl friend lived. My duffel bag had a large block M pasted on its side and I proudly sported a bronze "ruptured duck" honorable discharge pin in my lapel. Who could refuse a lift to a WWII vet going to college on the GI Bill? Well, plenty did just that at a traffic light crossroads in the city of Jackson about half way between Ann Arbor and Battle Creek. In fact I often waited for a lift there for hours until a truck driver in need of conversation to stay awake would pick me up. Only many years later was the mystery of the hitchhiker's dead zone solved when there appeared at that intersection a sign advising drivers on US 12 against picking up riders. Why? Because the state prison was only a couple of blocks away! This made me wonder why none of the drivers who dropped me off at that point had mentioned that fact. Probably didn't want to worry me, a war veteran trying to get through college on the G.I. Bill.

Hitchhiking may not be exclusively an American form of travel but it was seldom seen in Scandinavia when Bob Pierpoint and I decided to do some sightseeing in Norway after our 1947-1948 year of G.I. Bill study at the University of Stockholm. Our student caps and American flags attached to our back packs acted like magnets to attract Swedish drivers, most of whom had never met a real live American. We attended a dance in an outdoor pavilion in Mora and discovered to our dismay that the young ladies there lacked the "natural" beauty of the Swedish girls in Stockholm, who knew how to use makeup.

As we moved from the province of Dalarna into the foothills on the Norwegian border, vehicular traffic declined precipitously until a half hour passed between vehicles. At that point we waved down a bus headed in our northwesterly direction and climbed aboard. We soon realized that we had become the only passengers as we passed into Norway and the bus came to a stop at a little log inn at the southern end of Lake Femund. The driver asked if we were going to get off, and we said no, we're going to Trondheim. He said that was fine but this was the end of the road and we'd have to take a boat to proceed. We asked when the boat would leave, and he said "in a couple of days I think, but you'll have to ask in the inn down there by the water." This led to two wonderful days hiking and fishing for trout in the nearby rapids. Our guide was a 10-year-old boy whose gait suggested that he had learned to ski before he learned to walk. The innkeeper had relatives in the States and refused payment for our memorable stay on Lake Femund.

The little 60-foot steamer, piloted by a retired Norwegian-America Line skipper served as the only communication between the village settlements along the fifty mile lake shore and the outside world. We were met at each landing by everyone who lived within miles along the treeless shore to pick up their mail and handle other business. At one landing, a cow was brought aboard to be transported to the next landing where she would be serviced by the only bull in the area. A day or so later, we reached the northern end of Lake Femund where we spent the night in a cabin the main wall of which was covered with a huge American flag honoring an immigrant son.

H is for Hytta
by Austin Jay Goodrich

The Goodrich family, often joined with other relatives or friends, had many wonderful times at Skarvestølen (aka Hytta), the Norwegian side of the family's rustic log cabin nestled in the mountains of north-central Norway, despite the lack of creature comforts. There was no indoor plumbing or electricity. Water was obtained from a creek that ran a hundred yards behind the cabin. When the creek was covered with ice from October to April residents had to dig down through several feet of snow to get at it.

How could it be located? Well, believe it or not: you could hear it!

llumination was supplied by kerosene lamps and candles. What a warm living light those kerosene lamps provided. Water was heated on a large iron stove that doubled as a heat source for the main room, which had a large soapstone fireplace to warm the house around the clock. The W/C was a two-seater outhouse with scary trolls painted on the door and walls. Needless to say, the kids made every effort not to "go" after bed time for fear of things that went boom in the night. The W/C was a part of an outbuilding, which also had a garage, wood bin, washroom, and sauna, and a mysterious room that was always kept locked.

We usually spent a week there either to enjoy the snow-covered Easter holidays or round-the clock sunbathed summer vacations. Both seasons had their special charms and festivities, for kids and adults alike. During Easter holidays that lasted nearly a week there was skiing, jumping into snow banks three feet tall after twenty minutes in the sauna, building forts out of snow, throwing our arms out with snowballs, listening to Norwegian folk tales read by Mom by the warming fire, playing board games in the soft light of kerosene lamps, and sitting on the porch steps to soak up strong rays of sun giving promise of long summer days to come.

One spring, Dad woke me early, and urging quiet, told me to dress quickly and warmly, and meet him in the vestibule, where our ski apparel and boots were stored. We stole out into the first glimmer of dawn, and skied to the east, stopping on top of a hill with a glorious view of the frozen lake below us. There, with the sun just showing its face, we had our Father and Son talk. Having just finished a six week sex-ed program at school, I didn't have any questions about the mechanics, so we talked a lot about love and commitment, and being true to yourself and your spouse, which he said was really the same thing. What a wonderful way that was to start the day!

Another cherished memory was of the five days I spent in the cabin eight years later with my cousin Bibi, her husband Bjorn, and their wonderful children Cecelie, Christian, and Emil. Bibi was older than I by some years, enough so that she had in the past watched over me while visiting us in Holland and the States. Also old enough for me to develop a lifelong crush on her: she was (and is) in this boy's mind, the perfect woman. Smart, sweet, caring, lovely, and full of good humor, I'm afraid she set the bar too high for the women I met later in life. Cecelia, so open and curious about the world around her, and so much like her mother. Christian, so earnest and frank and fearless. Emil, the dreamer and playful imp. What a time I had enjoying their company that week – the fun we had!

In the summer there was hiking, mountain climbing, sailing handmade wood boats down the fossen (falls), Hoppa så Gossa (a strange dance performed by a group hand-in-hand prior to dropping their bottoms into frigid waters), and Lang-lang-rekke, a skipping game best enjoyed by a family of six, where as you sing the song and reach the climax, the person on the far right drops back and moves to join the line on the far left. It may not sound like much, but I can't remember laughing harder ever in my life. Those were sweet times indeed!

One summer, when I was thirteen and my brother Timo was nine, the two of us and Dad ventured out to conquer the mighty heights (3,300 feet) of Mount Mellon. Many had gone before us, and the trip up was mundane though beautiful and fun. After a sandwich and a shared Ringnes Export beer, Timo the Fearless suggested we travel down by the front of the mountain. This was not something often done, and I think were it not for the altitude (and the beer?), Dad would not have agreed to it. We started down, and made it safely to the bottom, though Dad later shared with me that he had seen a small sapling felled by a rock slide that was still green! Having worked up a good sweat, we doffed our clothes and enjoyed a brief skinny dip in the icy bright green waters of the snow fed lake at the base. Just as we were ready to exit the bone-chilling water, a couple of tourists decided to stop and say hello. Unaware of our naked state, they talked for several minutes, until they noticed our violent shivering and made a gracious exit. There was at least one man and two boys who slept like logs that night.

So I say thank you Hytta, and tusen takk to all those who shared it with me.

I is for Iceland

Of the scores of geographical misnomers, two of the most blatant appear in the region of the North Atlantic Ocean. Greenland, is a huge land mass covered with white snow, while Iceland is for most of the year clothed in green with little or no ice in sight.

On my first visit to Reykjavik, capital city of the Republic of Iceland, I had departed from Oslo, Norway in a blinding snowstorm. Much to my amazement, my plane landed at Reykjavik in the middle of the night with no snow to be seen on the runway or any place else at the airport. I thought, wow, the people of Iceland sure know how to handle the snow that must have covered their country by the time of my arrival in the middle of January. When I got up and peered out the window at my hotel the following morning my surprise turned to utter disbelief tinged with a sense of geographical disorientation. There stood the city square with a statue in its center and on one side a stately red brick building, which according to my tourist handbook, had to be the Ting (Thing), the oldest parliament in the entire world. But, strangely, there was not a trace of ice or a single fleck of snow to be seen anywhere.

(In a single flash of recall I imagined myself looking out of a hotel window in Kuching, capital city of the Indonesian island of Sarawak on the other side of the world where the inhabitants have never seen - nor will they ever see - snow. And it occurred to me that this might be an early warning signal for me to get into another line of work, where I might be able to experience new perceptions free of historical- recall pollution.

The object of my visit was the son of a leader of the Communist Party of Iceland, who was expected to rise to the top of the large communist party's hierarchy despite the usual ban against nepotism in the party leadership. It was easy to set up a meeting with the young man who seemed pleased to meet me, the first American he had ever met. We had dinner served in my room, and as I was about to make my pitch, a call for my guest came from the front desk. After a brief conversation in his native tongue, Thor Someone's son (I can't recall his family - actually father's name -) announced that he'd have to leave for an hour or so to help with a rescue operation involving a wreck of a fishing boat a few miles down the beach. I'd had meetings interrupted

45

by unscheduled occurrences before, but this was the first one to be put on hold by a shipwreck.

After he returned to our meeting, I made my pitch for him to meet secretly with my colleague in the U.S. Consulate to which my guest readily agreed. The gist of this approach focused on the need of the U.S. Government for accurate information on the intentions of the Communist Party of the Soviet Union. We were not interested in collecting information on the Icelandic Communist Party, but only on Soviet policy intentions on the global scene as reflected in their secret plans revealed to the inner circle of Icelandic communist party cadre.

Strange as it may seem, CIA's agents operating within the inner circles of national communist parties supplied some of the Agency's most valuable intelligence on Soviet foreign policy plans. The size of the national communist party didn't matter. As first among equals in the world's family of communist parties, the Soviet Union felt duty bound to keep its satellite parties informed, and we simply listened in via communist party penetration agents.

J is for Jay

Like both his sisters, this first-born son of Austin and Eva Goodrich arrived in Helsinki, Finland, in October, a time of year least often recommended for childbirth at the northern latitudes, because of the lack of vitamin-C loaded sunshine during the winter months. This deficiency was partially offset by getting the infant out in whatever sunshine was available. This compulsory exposure to outdoor air - the only kind worth breathing - turned Jay into a lifetime fresh-air freak along with his sisters, who were born in Sweden during the frigid months of winter.

Dr. Ruohankoski, the American-trained doctor who delivered Austin Jay in a Helsinki hospital a few blocks from where we lived in an apartment overlooking the city's beautiful harbor, quickly diagnosed our son's only health problem as geographical. His stomach was turned upside down, which made it impossible for him to digest food, even his mother's milk. The solution was both reasonable and simple: hold baby upside down and shake vigorously. The organ returned to its proper location and remained forever filled.

Jay's love of the outdoors was a mixed blessing. In the Dutch village of Voorburg, outside The Hague, he took his dog Suzy for a walk in 1960 that led them onto the railroad track bridge over Het Vliet canal. The local station master rescued them from being run over by the Rotterdam-Amsterdam express train. Some days later Suzy and her master continued their adventures by jumping into the feeder canal behind our house, which triggered a minor flood when our XXL maid, Cobi, hurdled into the water to rescue them. After a year in Voorburg, we moved into The Hague, capital of the Netherlands, where we lived happily in a red brick house, the only residential style employed by Dutch architects, on the Prinsevinkenpark a few blocks from the Peace Palace and the beach resort village of Scheveningen. (Try pronouncing this place name without sounding like a Maytag washing machine in dire need of repair.) It was there that Jay used to lead a band of little urchins to the candy store for a treat as his guests. For a few pennies, one could buy a hanful of snoopjes (candy). Where did Jay come buy his money? Why, the same place where I used to find small change to sate my appetite for candy: In mother's desk drawer.

Among the many memorable experiences I've shared with Jay is the way we set a world's record which I'm quite certain will never be broken. After we had been fishing for salmon just down stream from the Maalselv River falls in the province of Troms above the Arctic Circle in Norway for a couple of hours without a nibble, it occurred to us that these spawning fish had something other than food on their minds. It was getting warm in the sun so we decided to cool off in the waters of the fast-moving river. Our dip in the icy water lasted only so long as it took to scramble back up on the river bank and into our clothes. Years later, when I told an old salt I met on the docks in Narvik of our Arctic dip he simply shook his head and said "Nobody's ever done that and lived to tell about it." Well, Jay and I did and I'm here to tell about it.

Another memorable experience I shared with Jay came a dozen years later when he and his kid brother Timothy Lance (aka Timo) joined with me and two Norwegian carpenters to erect in three weeks time the imported log cabins in which our family lived very happily for a decade in Great Falls, Virginia. The Norse carpenters (Svein and Augun), the strongest men I've ever known (they carried the huge fir logs like toothpicks), had a great time driving around in our second car, a worn-out Olds 98. For some years, Jay and Timo lived in the *Veslebur*, a separate 10x15 foot log cabin set off from the main house and licensed as a shed for storage and laundry. (This permitted the installation of a toilet, shower and electricity in the building which couldn't be issued a permit for human habitation.) As a separate structure the boys could have their own private toilet facilities and play their hi-fi music at peak volume. And they could come and go with the night owls without disturbing their parents!

After the birth of our two red-headed daughters, Vesla and I were blessed to receive into our family a baby of the male gender we named Austin Jay. I have to confess that, as much as I disliked the idea of having a *Junior* offspring, I did like the idea of having a male child who would carry my name. So we named him Jay Austin and called him *Jay* after an early American hero named John Jay. Nevertheless, the boy somehow became known among his peers as Austin, even thought his parents and siblings continued to call him Jay. I suppose this underscores the relative unimportance of parental preference in matters as deeply personal as what name a person prefers to be called. And I suppose I was secretly proud that my first-born son liked to be called by my name.

Like his sisters, Austin Jay arrived in the early winter, indisputably the least desirable time of year for any baby to be born in the northern latitudes where the darkest months of winter severely shorten the hours of sunshine. Like all natives of the far north regions these babies received daily doses of C-loaded fish-liver oil and as much C-loaded sunshine as possible. To achieve this purpose, all three infants were put outdoors in buggies bundled up in eiderdown comforters to soak up as much of the healthy rays of sunshine as might become available.

Their addiction to sunshine as infants stuck with Jay and his siblings into their adult lives. I recall with great pleasure how Jay and I took a father-and-son vacation in the land of the midnight sun above the Arctic Circle in Norway. We bunked in a small cabin near a roaring waterfall (*fossen*) on the Namsos River, but spent very few hours a day sleeping. We hiked along the banks of the river and spent hours casting for salmon, most of whom who were en route to their spawning grounds above the falls. One day in the late afternoon we whimsically decided to strip off our clothes and take a dip in the fast-moving river downstream from the falls. It didn't last long, maybe half a minute tops. (When I later told a native in nearby Tromsoe about our impetuous swim, he just shook his head and said "Nobody ever swims in the water up here." Well, we did, but I must admit that neither of us will ever do it again.)

The innkeeper was disappointed that we'd been unable to catch any fish in his river. The Swiss tourists who rented the rights to fish in the pool below the falls caught tons of salmon, which they packed in ice in the trunks of their Mercedes to take back to serve in their restaurants in Geneva. (Maybe that's why I developed a particular loathing for this neutral nation of shopkeepers.) On the day of our departure, the innkeeper saw to it that we'd catch a salmon before leaving his area. His son, nicknamed "Skipper," who had the world's best job (shepherding rich widows on Caribbean cruise liners in the winter and goofing off at home in the fjord-studded paradise of northern Norway in the summers) drove us to a fishing boat in the port city of Tromsoe. We sailed out into the fjord where Jay landed a five kilo (12 lb.) salmon, which the hotel refrigerated overnight in preparation for our historic thousand mile train-foot-taxi journey to rejoin the family in the Rosenberg mountain retreat. En route from Oslo airport to the railway station we stopped at a butcher's shop to get The Fish repacked in fresh ice. Four hours later we caught a taxi in Fagernes to drive us and our precious cargo into the mountains in time for dinner at the family's "Skarvestoelen" log cabin retreat. Froeken Fjuk boiled the Fish and we ate it with boiled potatoes, pickled cucumbers and melted butter – the only way that the king of fish should ever be prepared for the table. Vesla's father, Bjarne Rosenberg, proclaimed it *den bedste malltid jeg har noensin smakt* (the best meal I've ever eaten). Jay beamed with pride.

Some years later, Jay returned to Oslo where he worked for a year at Rodeloekken Masjinverksted A/S, the Rosenberg family-owned machine shop factory, which manufactured railway switching equipment for the Norwegian State Railways. He returned home without a cent in his blue jeans.. I was poignantly reminded of how I returned from my year of study under the G.I. Bill of Rights program at the University of Stockholm (1947-48) flat-ass broke. While the cab that delivered me from the railway station in Battle Creek stood waiting outside our house at 38 Elizabeth Street, I greeted my Dad by asking him for a couple of bucks to pay off the taxi.

As they say: *Plus ca change, plus ca meme chose.* (The more things change the more they remain the same.)

K is for "K" Company

Company K of the 342nd Regiment, like all units of the 86th "Blackhawk" Infantry Division, represented an unusual mix of personnel. In contrast to the traditional hierarchical structure of military organizations - and society as a whole - the 86th was composed at its lower ranks with bright young men headed for college or the Air Force when World War II sidetracked their early-adult lives. (The 86th became known as the "kids division.") The non-commissioned officer ranks were occupied by older men who had been forced to leave school at a young age to help support their families. Street smarts were in command of scholars, future engineers, doctors and lawyers. I remember one Private First Class in L Company who had been an Assistant Attorney General in Ohio in civilian life. The upside-down ranking order might have been viewed as a recipe for disaster in the military? But somehow or other it worked. Only in America!

Perhaps the uniquely American inverted ranking order that characterized our Blackhawk composition is best described by Chuck "Bernie" Bernstein in his memoir *Blackhawk Mission: From Europe to the Pacific in World War II:*

"The U.S. Army is a uniform olive-drab unit trained 'by the numbers' to eat, sleep, work, play and fight together as one. Each of its parts was meant to be as homogenized as a Super Market carton of Grade A milk. Yet despite intense conformity training, the diversity of each GI's background, his culture, education, geographical idiomatic expressions, mirrored a diverse America."

My 4th (weapons) platoon of K Company was composed of one section of two 60- mm mortar squads, and one section of two light (.30 cal) machine gun squads. The platoon leader was a Second Lieutenant, a so-called *90-day wonder,* a graduate of Officer Training School, assisted by older non-commissioned officers each leading two squads of 6-8 men each. (I use the term "men" in a broad sense, since these privates and privates first class at the bottom of the rank ladder were all just 18 or 19 yeas old).

My squad leader, Victor "Vic" Renda, was an old (over 30) man, whose minimal formal schooling was more than compensated by street smarts acquired by operating poker and other illegal tables in his brother's gambling house in Des Moines, Iowa. Vic's acute survival skills in the army were matched by his dealing with a serious marital problem that arose during a week's furlough. After his return to Camp Livingston, Vic told me how he had taken advantage of his wife's brief absence on a shopping tour to become intimate with her sister, which left him with a case of the clap. It was my sergeant's challenging duty to keep this little secret – and its transmittal to his wife – by avoiding sexual contact with her for an unprecedented seven days. Vic's recounting of how he managed this feat kept me in stitches for a week.

My assistant machine-gunner, Steve Jarvis from New Jersey, was headed for an advanced math degree at Columbia University when military service called. Steve's idea of entertainment on weekends was to go into town and listen to classical music in record shops. He was accompanied on these musical expeditions by platoon mate John List, who some 25 years later murdered his mother, wife and three children before escaping to Colorado where he lived until captured and imprisoned until his death in 2008. John was officially diagnosed as the victim of post traumatic stress disorder acquired during the war, but this came to light too late to serve as an effective defense for his mass murder of his family. (See my biography of List, *Collateral Damage*, iUniverse, 2006.)

My outfit, the 86th Blackhawk Division was a one-of-a-kind infantry population. At its lowest level were boys with IQs above 120 who had been headed for college in the ASTP program or as Air Force cadets. The non-commissioned officer command levels were staffed with older men most of whom hadn't got beyond sixth grade. To spare them embarrassment, their IQ's will not be recorded here.

It was Plato's Utopia turned upside down, with the smartest and best educated at the bottom of the ladder and the less educated men in command. One might well view this as a recipe for disaster. But somehow - only in America - it worked. The schoolroom smarts at the bottom somehow blended with the street smarts of those ranked above them to produce an effective fighting force, a combat infantry unit that won the praise of all of the generals under whom they served, including Omar Bradley and George Patton.

My recollection of one of our platoon members, Ed Wandtke, may shed some light on how our upside-down personnel structure worked in practice. Ed's grandfather had been an *Uhlan* (lancer) in the Prussian Army and some of this military allegiance had been squeezed down through two generations. Unlike most of us, Ed actually liked army life and planned to make a career of it after the war. This plan was viewed as sheer lunacy by his comrades, even though two of Ed's platoon mates did re-up during the Koran war, but as commissioned officers. The aforementioned Lothrop Mittenthal was one. The other was John List, who in 1971 shot and killed his mother, wife and three teenage children and was later officially diagnosed as suffering from Post Traumatic Stress Disorder incurred during the war. (More on that tragedy below.)

Regardless of how Ed Wandke had come by his damaged genes, his platoon mates agreed unanimously that early intensive therapy would be needed to cure his disorder. Otherwise, Ed's deranged attitude might undermine the unity and morale of the platoon and, worse, offer encouragement to our officers and non-com oppressors. The educational process began one evening at 1900 Hours when Ed retired, saying he had a headache and would we please leave the hut so he could get some shut-eye. About twenty minutes later a voice yelled in the door, "Get up, Ed, Sgt Ramsey wants to see you! Platoon Sgt. Ramsey was Regular Army, a West Virginia mountain man who knew how to bank the coals in our pot-bellied stove at night to break through at exactly five the next morning. He also knew how to strip his troops of their meager paychecks in *"friendly"* poker games played with his deck of cards on top of his footlocker on paydays.

Just such a game was in progress when Ed appeared at the door of his hut dressed in Class-A uniform, including necktie. Ramsey looked up from his cards just long enough to rumble "Naw, I don't wanna to see you. Git outta here." Fifteen minutes later another voice called out to Ed. "Go to the Day Room, Wandke. You gotta make up a class in chemical warfare." Burned once, Ed went back to sleep. Ten minutes later an angry lieutenant appeared at the door and demanded to know in a loud voice why Ed had refused to obey orders. Ed ran to the Day Room where he spent an hour listening to fatuous information on CW, after which he staggered back to his bunk.

About 20 minutes later, three of Pfc Wandtke's comrades rousted him to obey an order to accompany them on a walk to the ordnance repair shop to pick up a mortar. Although a 60 mm mortar weighed only forty pounds and could easily be carried by one man, Wandtke was not one to argue that his presence on the detail was unneeded. After all, orders are orders, and Ed was not about to disobey a major tenet of the military philosophy he had embraced.

When the detail arrived at the ordnance depot it was closed and the troops started to walk a mile and a half back to their K Company huts in the dead of night. About half way back, Ed suddenly began to lurch about, moaning and groaning. Then he abruptly laid down in the middle of the road and began to cry. His headache by then had reached Vesuvian heights and all of the injustices of military life suddenly closed in on him. Pfc Wandtke swore a great oath to the effect that from day forward he would be a world class opponent of the Army and everything about it, including its discipline.

His re-humanizing education was complete and all of Ed's buddies welcomed his return to normalcy as a most positive development. Henceforth we privates could present a solid phalanx to the powers that were. Even the officers and non-coms were pleased, as they could now understand Ed's world view.

All things considered, I'm proud to say that I was an infantryman, one of the thirty percent of soldiers in the US Army who suffered seventy percent of total casualties in World War II. Some of those casualties were accidental, but nonetheless final. Some of them haunt my memory more than sixty years after they happened. I remember....

As we were preparing to move up to the front on the Rhine River outside the cathedral city of Cologne, we'd just been issued live ammunition and were busy cleaning our weapons. My assistant light (.30 calibre) machine gunner, Steve Jarvis, had just finished cleaning his side arm, a so-called "grease gun." This .45 caliber weapon was both easy to operate and cost only $9.99 cents to manufacture. Well, as they say, you get what you pay for. You could never hit your target with the M-3 unless you were aiming at the sky, because the gun rose up quickly, uncontrollably, when fired. There was another problem with this bargain-basement weapon. After cleaning it, there was only one way to move the bolt forward to close it, and that was to pull the trigger. If you did this when a loaded magazine was in place the weapon automatically fired.

That's how Steve accidentally shot our squad's ammo-bearer Joe Vittrano, who was seated just a few feet away in the upstairs bedroom of a German house cleaning his sidearm. Joe would have been killed but for a pocket Bible he carried in his shirt pocket. The lethal .45 caliber bullet bounced off Joe's good book and ricocheted down and out of his arm. We all assumed that Joe would be sewn up and given a medical discharge. No such luck. A few guys ran into him about eight months later in the Philippines, but the man who shot him never saw him again though he had tried to find him to apologize after the war ended. Later Steve wrote to tell me that he had not been able to locate his accidental victim, but that the incident continued to give him terrible fits of depression, nightmares and trouble sleeping.

The hand grenade was another weapon that killed friend and foe alike. We had just been issued grenades - four to a customer – as we prepared to move into battle in a mountain town in the Ruhr. We had heard that the cool thing to do was to loosen the crimped ends of the ring wire that held the handle in place and prevented the grenade from exploding prematurely. Everyone did this. Unfortunately a rifleman in the first platoon loosened the mechanism a little too much before attaching the grenade to his back pack. When he shifted his weight as he relaxed outside the village church, the pin fell out and the grenade hissed into life before ending the life of Pfc Muldoon exactly four and a half seconds later. I returned to my foxhole and buried my grenades after deciding that it might be safer to take my chances of surviving the war without them.

Then there was the day in mid March 1945 when we came under the so-called "friendly fire" of our own artillery. We had marched all day and were taking a break in a pine forest above the church town of Hilchenbach in preparation for our first night attack. Artillery shells were heard lazily crossing overhead as the bombardment began to soften resistance to our scheduled attack. No one paid any attention. We'd only been in combat for a couple of weeks, but we knew that the shell you could hear wouldn't hurt you, didn't have your name on it. Word was passed not to worry, "it's friendly fire." This reassurance became less comforting as the shells kept getting lower in the sky, louder and closer to the tall evergreens rising above us. Then it happened. Six or eight or maybe a dozen shells exploded right over our heads. All hell broke loose.

Surely tree-hugging became habitual that night. The ground was too hard to dig in so I tried to save my ass by becoming a part of a tall pine tree. And I prayed for God to make 'em stop. "Please God," I begged.

Then very suddenly a terrible silence wrapped in a sour-sweet cloud of cordite descended on our hillside. Through the calls for "Medic, medic, over here, medic," I heard a call that continues to haunt my memory. I heard it only once. It was Pfc Marks, a teen-aged rifleman in the 3rd platoon, a practical joker whose face was always smiling, as if he'd just pulled off a successful prank. He had called out one word: "Mother."

Years later at a Blackhawk Division reunion I ran into the medic fittingly named "Joe Medich," who had tried to treat Marx' wounds, and I asked him about our comrade's dying call for his mother. He must have seen her in his mind's eye," I ventured.

"Well, no," said Joe. "Because Joe never saw his mother."

"How's that," I asked.

"Well, you see, Joe told me years ago that his mom died in childbirth."

* * * * * * * *

After moving into the town of Hilchenbach late at night, we found the place occupied by battle-hardened troops of the Panzer Lehr Division, who acted like they owned the place, which I guess they did since they were Germans in Germany, marching through *their* streets and shouting orders in *their* language as we sat silently, shivering in the cold of *their* houses. The next morning, a detail of "volunteers" from my Fourth Platoon was sent back into the woods to retrieve the men who had been wounded and killed there by our own "friendly fire" the night before. They were all captured and held prisoners for a day or two by German troops.

One member of this detail was John List. It was John List, who 25 years after the war took a war souvenir pistol in hand and shot and killed his mother, his wife and their three teen-aged children. After living under an assumed name in Colorado for about 20 years, and remarrying, John was captured as the result of his appearance on the America's Most Wanted TV show. He was sentenced to serve five consecutive life sentences when he died of natural causes on a Good Friday in 1998. I corresponded with John and helped write his memoirs (Collateral Damage, iUniverse, 2006.) An interesting sidelight on the life of John List is this: He was officially diagnosed as suffering from post traumatic stress disorder for which he received treatment and disability compensation from the Veterans Administration. Could this medical condition explain why John List, the most gentle person I have ever known, became a family murderer? This question was addressed by the judge who passed judgment on John. He claimed that List's army combat was an irrelevant issue, because when he was questioned by a psychiatrist, John could not remember any details of his combat experience. The sad fact is that the blocking out of traumatic experiences is a hallmark symptom of post traumatic stress disorder. Were John List and his murdered family members victims of this disorder. Were they collateral damage of war? Yes, I believe they were.

Back to the subject of fighting in the Ruhr pocket. There was humor as well as tragedy. During a fierce fire fight in the city of Ludenscheid, right in the middle of the city square, an apartment house door was suddenly thrown open and a German business man emerged. With his umbrella raised on high and his briefcase on top of his head, the man shouted "*sivilist*" (civilian) and jogged across the street explaining that it was necessary for him to get to his office, so could we please stop all the shooting there on his street, the *hauptstrasse* of Ludenscheid.

Another bittersweet memory of mine stems from a small bungalow where we were earlier billeted on the outskirts of Cologne. As I lay on a small bed trying to get some sleep my eyes were drawn to a needlepoint wall hanging. It read:

Ich bin klein, mein hertz mach rein;
Soll nieman dritt wohnen als Jesu allein.

Which translates to;
"I am small, make my heart clean, So no one will live there but Jesus alone."

My mother had taught me this prayer when I was a little kid. The absolute madness of war made a chill run through my body. Here I was in Germany, the homeland of my father's family, reading a child's prayer I had learned as a kid from my mom. Here I was about to move across the Rhine River and kill as many of my distant relatives as possible. Crazy? Yes. There's no other word for war.

Actually I didn't kill nearly as many Germans as I took prisoner. Most of the Wehrmacht soldiers knew they were beaten and were only too happy to surrender to the Americans. The Red Army on the eastern front didn't take prisoners. One evening I was on guard duty at a fenced enclosure that contained several thousand German G.I.'s when I heard a voice from the other side of the barbed wire.

"Excuse me. Mister, I'm down here."

I looked through the wire to see a baby-faced kid in a gray Wehrmacht uniform.

"Whatcha want?" I growled. We weren't supposed to talk with prisoners.

"I, uh, I'm an American."

"The hell you say. What are you doing in a German uniform?"

"Well, see, years go, I came over here with my parents to visit family in Hungary. Then the war started and we couldn't leave to go home to America."

I looked down to see tears in the eyes of this kid, who had been drafted into a Wehrmacht Labor Battalion as a pre-teen American citizen!

"I'll see what I can do," I said, and gave him a chocolate bar from my K ration.

After the Ruhr, we joined Patton's Third Army and raced southeast all the way to the Danube River. We hated ol' Blood and Guts, General George Patton. He moved so fast, we never got any sleep, never had a decent meal, never got to take a shower, never got clean clothes. (I went through a month of combat wearing some German civilian's black pants after mine were shredded getting through a barbed wire fence in the Ruhr Pocket.)

Only years later did I realize that I owed my life to Gen Patton, who moved so fast that the enemy never knew where we were coming from. Finally, deep in Bavaria we did encounter some heavy resistance mainly from diehard SS troops and members of the grounded Luftwaffe.

Another threat to our good health and, more especially, our peace of mind was posed by the enemy's anti-tank/anti-aircraft artillery, the eighty-eights (88 millimeter caliber). These canons had the muzzle velocity of rifles, which produced a blood-chilling effect when they screamed a few feet over your head.

In an effort to avoid them, I had found refuge in an abandoned German fox hole in Ingolstadt next to a demolished railway bridge on the banks of the Danube River. Suddenly something metallic bounced off my helmet and I thought I'd bought the farm for sure. As it turned out, the object was a .50 caliber shell casing that had fallen from an American F-47 fighter plane strafing a farm shed that might have been an enemy observation post on the other side of the river.

At sundown, just when we had hopes of getting a night's sleep in a nearby apartment house, the order came down that we were to be the first troops to cross the Danube River. We were told that General Patton himself had issued the order, as if that would make it more popular with his dog-tired troops who wanted nothing more than an undisturbed night's sleep. We dragged the wooden skiffs that had been dumped off by trucks that didn't hang around very long, down to the river bank, where we jumped in and began to paddle for all we were worth. We had no idea what awaited on the far shore, but it couldn't be worse than what we were leaving behind.

When we reached the other shore I jumped out and helped my squad leader, Vic Renda, who didn't know how to swim, to get a foothold on the slippery river bank. At the same time I had to hold on to the boat in a swift current. Since I had only two hands, something had to go. My machine gun disappeared in the muddy waters of a river misnamed the *blue* Danube. After another guy got hold of a tree on the muddy river bank, I dove into the icy waters to retrieve my gun.

And I want to tell you, that sitting in a foxhole that night, soaking wet, was not the most pleasant experience I've ever had. But it was by far the coldest one. It was even more unpleasant for the troops who were drowned in the river, and there were many, including our Executive Officer, "Red" Brown..

At one point a comrade I recognized by his voice as the Captain of L Company came stumbling along the river bank asking in a loud whisper if we had seen anyone from "L" Company. We hadn't. The company commander couldn't locate a single one of the hundred plus members of his command. Now *that's* really "missing in action."

A week later, after crossing the Isar River and the Isar Mittel canal, we had a fierce encounter with some tough German troops in the town of Berglern. (Years later, our entire company were awarded Bronze Stars for that action.) I had used up all of my ammunition when the call came for me to provide covering fire so that our medic could reach our beloved company commander, Captain Macalester, who lay wounded in a nearby field. And I was out of ammunition. Captain Mac, who preferred marching straight ahead under enemy fire instead of taking cover - a tactic known as marching fire - died trying to end the war as soon as possible, and to this day I blame myself for not being able to help save him. There's a whole bunch of guilt in war. Some lasts a lifetime.

After the war in Europe ended, we were returned home, given a two weeks furlough and a couple of weeks training at Camp Gruber OK, before being rushed onto troop ships in San Francisco bound for the Pacific Theatre of Operations to help win *that* war. It turns out that we were slated to be among the first troops to invade the main islands of Japan. Fortunately President Truman ordered the atomic bomb to be dropped, and very suddenly, blessedly, the war came to an end. (Some historical revisionists maintain that Mr. Truman should never have dropped that bomb, that we could have won the war without it. But there is compelling evidence that the Japanese were prepared to fight to the death to defend their home islands and that victory without the bomb could only have been won at a terrible price, including most certainly my own life and, more importantly, the precious lives of my children. And their children.

Austin Goodrich
Age 16 · Jr · Wt 169 · Tackle · 38 Elizabeth

Battle Creek Bearcats All-State Tackle (offense and defense!)

"Red" on furlough from Camp Livingston, LA (1944)

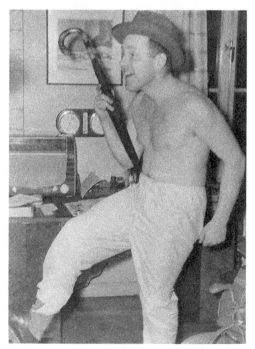

Dancing bachelor in his student apartment
in Stockholm, Sweden (1948)

Trout caught in Norwegian Mountain stream

Cyrus and Austin at Battle Creek Airport

Swimming in mountain pool with Britt

Dad and daughters out for a walk

Mormor and Vesla with baby Tina in Oslo, Norway

Austin interviewing Ingrid Bergman after her
performance of *Joan of Arc* in Stockholm

Tina (left) and Britt with their grandfather's
Bjarne's pipes in Ljan, Norway

Austin and Jay on Helsinki balcony

Vesla and Austin Jay at Skarvestølen cabin in Norwegian mountains

Austin and Timothy Lance (aka Timo) in Holland

Britt skating in Holland

Tina at the Amsterdam Zoo

Timo, Austin Jay with cousins Jonathan Guilbert,
Austy Guerin, and Rob Guilbert

Austin (dark glasses) with Bangkok touch football buddies (1967).

Timo and Jay hook a rickshaw ride in Hong Kong.

Bob Nelson and Austin aprés sauna bath at Skarvestølen, Vesla's family hytte in the Norwegian Mountains (Easter, 1971).

Timo and Tina enjoy Norway's great ice
cream cones in Fagernes (1971).

Tina atop Skarven — mountain in Oestre Slidre, Norway.

Etz, Ellie, Austin, Helen and Vesla outside the
Dancing Crab Restaurant in D.C.

Vesla, Bill Rollins, Tina, Britt and Gary Weaver
at backyard crab feast in Great Falls, VA

Timo, Marilyn Dale and Austin Jay at Great Falls, VA cabin.

Sammy gets a lift from skiing daddy in Hubertus, WI (1991)

Sammy and Mona outside Lake Park Bistro, Milwaukee, WI.

Etz, Helen, Ellie (seated), Austin and Eleanor celebrate
Eleanor's 80th birthday at the home of Rob and Jim.

Helen and Austin at Crystal Lake, MI.

Miscellaneous WW II Recollections:
The Re-humanization of Ed Wandtke

Ed's grandfather had been an *Uhlan* (lancer) in the Prussian Army and some of this military allegiance had been squeezed down through two generations. Unlike most of us, Ed actually liked the army life and planned to make a career of it after the war. This plan was viewed as sheer lunacy by his comrades, even though two of Ed's platoon mates did re-up during the Koran war, but as commissioned officers. The aforementioned Lothrop Mittenthal was one. The other was John List, who in 1971 shot and killed his mother, wife and three teenage children. None of his Blackhawk Division comrades could believe that this gentle person could ever commit such a crime. An explanation appeared in 2001 while he was serving a five consecutive life terms sentence in a New Jersey prison: John List was officially diagnosed as suffering from Post Traumatic Stress Disorder incurred during the war.

Regardless of how Ed Wandke had come by *his* damaged genes, his platoon mates agreed unanimously that early intensive therapy would be needed to cure his disorder. Otherwise, Ed's deranged attitude might undermine the unity and morale of the platoon and, worse, offer encouragement to our officers and non-com oppressors.

The educational process began one evening at 1900 Hours when Ed retired, saying he had a headache and would we please leave the hut so he could get some shuteye. About twenty minutes later a voice yelled in the door, "Get up, Ed, Sgt Ramsey wants to see you!" Platoon Sgt. Ramsey was Regular Army, a West Virginia mountain man who knew how to bank the coals in our pot-bellied stove at night to break through at exactly five the next morning. He also knew how to strip his troops of their meager paychecks in "friendly" poker games played with his deck of cards on top of his footlocker on paydays.

Just such a game was in progress when Ed appeared at the door of his hut dressed in Class-A uniform, including necktie. Ramsey looked up from his cards just long enough to rumble "Naw, I don't wanna see you. Git outta here.

Fifteen minutes later another voice called out to Ed. "Go to the Day Room, Wandtke. You gotta make up a class in chemical warfare." Burned once, Ed went back to sleep. Ten minutes later an angry lieutenant appeared at the door and demanded to know in a loud voice why Ed had refused to obey orders. Ed ran to the Day Room where he spent an hour listening to fatuous information on CW, after which he staggered back to his bunk.

About 20 minutes later, three of Pfc Wandtke's comrades rousted him to obey an order to accompany them on a walk to the ordnance repair shop to pick up a mortar. Although a 60 mm mortar weighed only forty pounds and could easily be carried by one man, Wandtke was not one to argue that his presence on the detail was unneeded. After all, orders are orders, and Ed was not about to go against a major tenet of his military philosophy.

When we arrived at the ordnance depot it was closed and we started to walk a mile and a half back to our K Company huts in the dead of night. About half way back, Ed suddenly began to lurch about, moaning and groaning. Then he suddenly lay down in the middle of the road and began to cry. His headache by then had reached Vesuvian heights and all of the injustices of military life suddenly closed in on him. Pfc Wandtke swore a great oath to the effect that from day forward he would be the world champ opponent of the Army.

His re-humanizing education was complete and all of Ed's buddies welcomed his return to normalcy as a most positive development. Henceforth we privates could present a solid phalanx to the powers that were. Even the officers and non-coms were pleased, as they could now understand Ed's world view.

Survivor's Guilt

by Alfred "Ted" Goodwin, 342nd 3rd Bn Hqs

In September of 1944, following the levy of both officers and EM to overseas replacement assignments in response to losses during the invasion of Normandy, and heavy casualties in the Pacific, the division at Camp Livingston, LA, received a significant number of ASTP enlisted men and new officers from Ft. Benning. About the same time, the still depleted enlisted and junior officer ranks were brought up to Table of Organization strength by "retreads" from the air force, the coast artillery, and other units, to be retrained by the 86th Division for amphibious operations in the Pacific.

Most of the new "ninety day wonders" were third year ROTC students who were still in training at Benning when 1944's heavy casualties were sustained overseas. My ROTC (Oregon) class of 1944, in peace time, would have been commissioned on the campus. Instead, we were mobilized in 1942, trained as infantrymen in 1943, and commissioned at OCS during stateside duty. These young officers were just a year or two older than the ASTP trainees who joined them as rookie Blackhawks during the fall of 1944. The 342nd Infantry that boarded the *Kungsholm* bound for Le Havre carried a lot of college kids in enlisted grades one and two, and a lot of shiny new gold bars on lieutenants fresh from ROTC and Fort Benning. The senior noncoms and company commanders, since Camp Howze, had been hand picked for retention during the repeated levies for replacements. The division was a good cross section of what Tom Brokaw later called "The Greatest Generation."

While we were still at Camp Livingston, Maj. Ward saw me in the I Co. area, sitting outside my hut with a portable typewriter, banging away on a letter home. He was in his jeep, with T/5 Vernon Moore driving, and stopped. I jumped up and saluted. He said, "Goodwin can you type?" I said "Yes, Sir!" The next thing I knew, he had me transferred from I Co., where First Sgt. Stafford was training me, over to 3rd. Bn. HQ Co. There I was assigned, on paper, to the Ammunition and Pioneer Platoon, and in fact, to a pile of army forms and a GI typewriter. Concurrent training as a powder monkey and as a clerk-typist filled the remaining days at Livingston. Assisting a gung-ho West

Pointer with his paper work, which he hated, was fun but stressful. In the field, or later, with the Navy on amphibious training, life was strictly demolition ammunition supply. When in garrison long enough to change clothes, it was the life of a "ball-bearing WAAC," typing up the major's reports. In 1990, at a high school class reunion, I told my typing teacher that she probably saved my life in Germany. Instead of leading a rifle platoon in marching fire, like my ROTC classmates, I was further back in the column, herding ammunition deuce and a halfs as calls came in for more mortar ammo and boxes of machine gun belts.

Sixty years later, I still carry a burden of survivor's guilt. The lieutenant who took my place in I Company was killed in the German mortar barrage that greeted the first platoon's crossing of the Danube. Lt. John Seaton was a class of '44 ROTC student from the University of Montana. Whenever someone brings up World War II, I think of John, the Big Sky he never got to see again, and of the random craziness of assignments and deployments when a nation goes to war.

L is for Lance Keyworth and Ljan, Norway

I met the man who became one of my life's very best friends in Helsinki, capital of Finland, one of the very best-kept secrets in Europe. The swarthy complexion of Lancelot Allan Keyworth bespoke an ethnic mix that might have included a touch of blood from colonial India, but in his dress, manners and bearing "Lance" was as English as Eton College, Buckingham Palace and the Tower of London rolled into one. I never knew and never asked how it was that this polished English gentleman came to settle in Helsinki where he ran a translation bureau and served as the Finnish correspondent for Time-Life and the Financial Times of London. Perhaps the answer rested with his charming wife, Ulla, widow of an Olympics 5,000-meter champion runner, a Finnish Army officer who was killed in the 1939-40 "Winter War" with the Soviet Union.

Lance founded and served as the first president of the Western Foreign Press Club, which was set up in Helsinki for the express purpose of distancing the foreign correspondents of western democracies from the state employees of Soviet bloc government-managed media. We met on Saturdays for lunch and a few bottles of A-Class (Atomic) beer first in the press room, then recessed to the bar on the ground floor of the old Kemp Hotel, which had once served as the chief hangout for Finnish composer Jean Sibelius and other cultural luminaries of the 20th century.

Later, when the old Kemp was torn down to make room for a new hotel and, regrettably, the loss of the octogenarian tux-clad string quartet in the dining room, Lance managed to move our Club meetings to the Kauppakilta - Commerce Club - a few blocks away. Two or three times a year club members were invited to tour Finnish plants interested in courting publicity and new customers in the United States and other western countries. Excluded from membership in western economic/trade organizations by the terms of their friendship treaties with the USSR, the Finns nevertheless managed to gain a large market in the western democracies, particularly for their paper products.

One reason for Finland's high credit rating was its timely repayment of foreign debts. In recognition of this unique record, Congress had ordered that all of the interest on these loans be used to fund the travel of Finnish and American students chosen for so-called Fulbright scholarships. I was honored to serve on the Finnish-American committee that awarded these travel grants. In proportion to their population, there were more college students studying in the U.S. from Finland than from any other country.

Years later, I complimented Dr. Voss-Hoeckert, a Finnish pediatrician and brother-in-law of Lance Keyworth who had supervised the treatment of our daughter Tina, for the skill and dedication displayed by of by Finnish doctors and nurses. He invited me to visit the staff lounge at the hospital which featured on its walls photographs of the doctors who served there. One by one, he identified them with the medical colleges in the United States where they had received medical training. "Much of the credit belongs to your country," he said. I silently nodded and left the room to conceal my proud and grateful tears.

Outside the Press Room on the second floor of the old Kemp Hotel, foreign correspondents were privileged to witness the annual First of May labor parades from a rickety perch on the front of the hotel's sand stone balcony. As communist and socialist workers marched under bright red flags on the street below, we stood on the balcony and raised our glasses in fraternal solidarity. The marchers glared up at us in a way that seemed to express their contempt for the ruling class and dedication to a revolution that would replace us. Thanks to a politically active labor movement throughout Scandinavia, the workers in that part of the world reached the balcony of political power via the peaceful road of economic democracy.

One of my fondest memories of Lance was the way he led us members of the Western Foreign Press Club on marches among tables in the Commerce Club and other Helsinki restaurants to the whistled stains of the Colonel Boogey march, as smiling Finnish diners raised their glasses in salute. I know of no other place in the world where this has - or ever could have - taken place.

When I lived in Norway in the summer of 1950, **Ljan** (pronounced Yahn) was no more than a local stop on the train service from Oslo, capital city of Norway, east to the Swedish border and on to the capital city of Stockholm, Sweden. In terms of my life it was much more than that. It was where my late wife, Eva "Vesla" nee Rosenberg, mother of our four wonderful children, lived in a grand white villa overlooking the headwaters of Oslo Fjord. It was the starting point of my long day's rail/bus journey across the border into Sweden to buy an engagement/ wedding ring to seal my proposal of marriage to Eva Benedikte Thue Rosenberg with whom I had fallen in love. (There was no gold to be had in war-devastated war Norway, but gold rings could be had in Sweden, which, like Switzerland, had remained neutral in the war.)

The sojourn served as a second test of the depth of my desire to wed Vesla. (The first and greater test was overcoming an Agency ban against staff employees marrying foreign nationals. I had to submit a formal petition for an exemption to this rule backed by my signed letter of resignation. Fortunately my resignation was turned down, for which I shall forever be grateful to the leadership of the Central Intelligence Agency.)

I departed on my marital journey in pre-dawn darkness, slipping and sliding down the icy path through the woods to the local Ljan train stop. At the border I switched to a bus to get to Karlskrona, where a jewelry store awaited. I bought our rings, and waited an hour to get them inscribed with our names and date of our engagement, which I incorrectly inscribed as December 31 1950. (As it turned out, when I got back to the Rosenberg home at 11 p,m. on December 30th, the place was ablaze in lights in anticipation of my return.)

After sharing the announcement with her family members, Vesla and I went out on the balcony to seal our marital pledge in the most wonderful setting in the world. Straight across the fjord that led to the North Sea and the rest of the world stood the Holmenkollen Olympics ski jump and to the right at the head of the fjord glittered the lights of an oversized village, that was Oslo, formerly known by its more lyrically pleasing Danish name of Kristiania. There may be more splendid natural settings for a city than this, but I don't know where they might be.

M is for Mona

I am eternally grateful to my slightly older sister, Eleanor Guilbert, for introducing me to the beautiful woman who became my wife and mother to our beloved daughter, Samantha. Mona Alyce Stender worked with Eleanor in the public relations office of the School Sisters of Saint Francis on the south side of Milwaukee. They were token Protestants in the Roman Catholic mission, whose members were ordained Nuns dressed mostly in traditional black and white clerical garments. They were nice people doing good works, which included the acclaimed paintings created by Sister Helena. A large oil canvas of a vase of peonies painted by this tiny, talented nun has blessed our living room wall for many years.

After dinner at Bob and Eleanor's home, Mona and I enjoyed an evening at one of Milwaukee's many small theatres. I don't recall what was staged – it may have been a Nowell Coward comedy – but that didn't matter because my attention was focused exclusively on my date. Mona was – and is – a beautiful woman endowed with the spontaneous charm of a young lady raised in the beautiful rolling hills and valleys of the glacier-sculpted Kettle Moraine countryside in southeastern Wisconsin less than an hour's drive north of Milwaukee. Her father, Harry, was an orphaned child endowed with an eyesight peculiarity that provided him with a special ability to interpret aerial photographs for the Air Force in WW II. With the aid of a G.I. loan, Harry opened an art supply retail store in Milwaukee and married Mona's beloved mother, Mary Kelar. The couple lived on a large farm that had a largely unused barn and a small chinked-log outbuilding heated by a small pot-bellied stove, which in later years served as my heated my office space and the site of poker games with my golf buddies.

After her first marriage ended in divorce, and her beloved mother died from a heart attack, Mona returned to live in her childhood home in Hubertus, WI, with her mixed breed Labrador dog, *Darby*. She and I fell deeply in love and after some time living together on the Hubertus farm and in an apartment in downtown (Third Ward) Milwaukee, we decided to be wed at our 100-year old New England-style Congregational Church in Richfield, WI. Reverend Alice Murphy presided, my son Austin Jay served as best man, and Mona's close friend and [Lawrence] college roommate Deborah Mell was maid of honor. We celebrated our marriage at the Richfield Country Club dining room at a banquet graced by the attendance of members of both families, and our beloved daughter Samantha Helen Stender Goodrich. (See under **S** for Samantha.)

For several years, Mona continued to work part-time at the School Sisters of St. Francis while her husband plonked away on his Underwood as a free lance writer in the log cabin and later at our residences in Franklin and Port Washington. Somehow, Mona managed to find time to provide our beloved daughter with a happy childhood filled with love and devotion enriched by happy family vacations in Scotland and Ireland. Her ability to raise and help support the material needs of a family enriched by world travel tells everything we need know of this truly wonderful woman. Mona combines in a word – love – all of the God-given qualities that enrich and glorify life on this earth.

N is for Nicknames

The people who grew up during the Depression years of the 1930's leading up to World War II were compensated for the lack of material wealth with a virtual gold mine of nicknames. Every one of us had at least two unofficial monikers (one gladly accepted and one more or less despised (in Italics) in addition to the names that appeared on our birth certificates. Some of us had three or four *noms de plum*. Here are some of them.

Name on Birth Certificate	Nickname(s)	Derivatrion
Eleanor Bjorseth	B.J.	Initials for unpronujcible family name
Howard Bivens (drugstore prop.)	Bee	Surname initial
Margaret Ann Corlett	Mac	From names' initials
David Crippen	Snorky	Snorkel nose shape
John Dodge	Demon Squint Eye	Bad actor repute Hooded eyes
Robert Galloup	Arrow	Fleetness afoot
John O. Galloup	Yutch Giddy / GiddyPoop	Cartoon character unknown
Donald Geyer	The Hare	Speed afoot (to catch naughty boys)
Austin Goodrich	The Hammer Red (in Army 1943-46) Cy or Sy	To punish them Hair/beard color Dad's nickname
Eleanor Austin Goodrich	Goody, Snag	Family name, For catching beaus
Robert Hamilton	Hambone, Hamfat Gooch Mayor's Son	Cartoon character Dad was Mayor
John Hoffman	Buck	Abbreviated name for drug to treat the clap
Robert Kuehnle	Kunkle, Keenabach	Phonetic/ethnic
Andrew Watson Lockton	Shysty Watt	Shyster (lawyer) plus shortened middle name.
Mulford Rose	Muff Potter	From Tom Sawyer
Russell Strand	Muscles Four Eyes	Toughest boy (Never used close up)
Robertr Wertz	Whirlwind (Whirly)	Football speed afoot

O is for Oslo

I guess I'd never have known anything about the capital city of Norway if my branch chief in CIA had not suggested that the best way to get to my assigned tour as a non-official cover (NOC) officer in Stockholm might be to first establish my Scandinavian presence in neighboring Oslo. He was right. When people in Sweden asked how it was that I came to their country, it was easy to explain that I came over from neighboring Norway. To explain how I came all the way from America would have required a much longer – and less credible - explanation. So it was that I and my car (a '46 Ford coupe) quietly returned to Scandinavia to attend a GI Bill supported summer school course for American students at the University of Oslo.

Oslo is quite simply the best place in the world to live. In the winter you can put on skies and navigate trails that surround the city. In summer you can sun and swim with or without a bathing suit in the glistening waters of the fjord; walk through downtown from the palace to the railroad station without breaking a sweat; and, take boat trips to island dance halls or to uninhabited skerries. My first residence in my low-profile life there was an outbuilding beside a shed that housed a dozen or so loud-mouthed chickens. My day started early with a naked dash down through the woods out into the icy waters of the fjord. What a great way to wake up!

Next I drove into town to attend summer school classes for American classmates or – more frequently – joined my landlord Thor Lund for three or four sets of tennis on courts owned by unseen neighbors. Later, I joined with my landlord's father to fish in the fjord for dinner using worms from his garden as bait. On a pivotal day in my life, I drove Thor and his wife, Eva, to the 100-meter stretch of open water that protected island inhabitants from unwanted visitors, to be drawn by an outboard-propelled barge across the inlet to the mainland. We drove up along the fjord wall half an hour to a large white adobe house where the Rosenberg family lived. We had been invited to *aftensmat* (an evening supper), which featured crawfish washed down with a few drams of Linie aquavit chased by excellent Norwegian beer to drown any inhibitions that may have impeded our conversation. Eva (aka *Vesla*) Rosenberg and I hit it off beautifully from this first meeting until we were married in Oslo the following spring. Vesla spent the winter in London studying English, and we kept in touch via mail and the airwaves. One might wonder how we could do this. Well, thanks to my University of Stockholm buddy, Bob Pierpoint, I was able to replace him as a news/feature reporter for Radio Sweden. (I also took Bob's job as the CBS Scandinavian correspondent when Bob got a staff job with CBS reporting from Korea and later became a stalwart on the CBS News staff until he retired to go fishing in California.) In London, Vesla was able to listen to my short-wave broadcasts on her roommate's receiver. These news-feature radio shows always contained short coded love messages. This use of my professional cover job to transmit coded love notes enhanced our relationship with the qualitative upgrade of secrecy, which has always served to spice up my life.

P is for Pseudonyms

Now there is an important difference, sports fans, between an official pseudonym and an operational alias one might use to protect ones true name from becoming known (blown) to persons unauthorized to know it. A pseudonym is the name that a CIA officer uses to sign official documents such as receipts for advances, accountings and reimbursement of operational expenses. When I first arrived in Washington to sign on for employment in CIA I was asked to register what would henceforth become my official name. It was James K. Abney (my training pseudo). Later this was changed to Joseph S. Tiffany. These were classy names, which I gladly accepted. Not all pseudos were this nice.

A secretary I knew was initially assigned the pseudo "Martha P. Crapsey." She appealed for - and got - a new name she could more easily live with.

To register my new official name I was asked to sign it a dozen times before making it official on a signature card. This procedure was my first official act as a staff employee of the Central Intelligence Agency performed in a room at the Statler Hotel In Washington, D. C. at a meeting for which I arrived precisely one hour late. That was because my train was running on eastern standard rather than daylight savings time. Great start, I thought, showing up an hour late for my first day in a career that put a premium on punctuality.

My official pseudo, James K. Abney, was many years later replaced (for some unknown reason) with Joseph S. Tiffany, another classy moniker.

In operational situations I used a variety of names chosen by myself and recorded in official correspondence with Headquarters. I chose these names from my own memory bank of friends so that I could quickly bring them to mind to avoid the embarrassment of appearing to forget my own name. I used Bob Gustke, John Lindberg and Edward "Fast Eddy" Sundberg, all of them backstopped with alias documentation for use in buying airline tickets, hotel registration and the like. Only once did my wife accompany me on an operational trip. It was on a trip to Paris, and she neglected to use my alias when she showed up for a hair appointment that had been made for her in my assumed name in which I was registered at the hotel. She was briefly embarrassed, but the hairdresser dismissed her memory lapse as an ordinary case of extra-marital name confusion. In France this was overlooked as a common mistake. No problem.

Sometimes I used an alias simply to avoid the problem of having my name misspelled by people making restaurant or theater reservations for me. For some reason, Goodrich never got recorded correctly. It got taken down as anything from Gothenburg to Gascrick. So I often used common, phonetically clear names familiar to the person who might be on the other end of the line. Thus, in Scandinavia I made reservations as Lund, Olson or Sundberg; in Germany I got quality service as Doktor Schmidt or Professor Rammel. The use of a title was mandatory if I wanted to make sure of getting a good seat at the theatre or table in a restaurant. I'm sure this still holds true.

P is for Port Washington

After making more than two dozen *permanent* changes of address on this planet, I sailed into the new millennium with Mona and our daughter, Samantha, in Port Washington, Wisconsin. This scenic fishing village on Lake Michigan about 30 miles north of Milwaukee is inhabited by 10,000 solid citizens, many of them with family roots that stretch back to Belgium and Luxemburg. The city's largest employer, the Chair Company, shut down many years ago. Then the large Simplicity lawn mower factory moved south in pursuit of higher profits derived from reduced labor costs. (I wonder if labor representation on corporate boards as legally required in Scandinavia might reduce the profoundly damaging effects that moves of this magnitude inevitably have on the lives of the companies' families).

Despite its loss of factories and the closure of the city's famous seafood restaurant, Smith Brothers, which attracted diners from Milwaukee and even Chicago, Port Washington remains a geographically scenic and vibrant community. Its schools produce an unusually high level of education, including world class programs in music and theatre. When our daughter Samantha Helen Stender Goodrich matriculated at the University of 'Wisconsin – Milwaukee, her drama teachers were profoundly impressed with the list of the roles she had played in high school theater prductions.

Personally, I have found profound pleasure in the people-friendly atmosphere of this city. On occasion when this octogenarian who should have known better has taken to his cross-country skis in the Upper Lake Park and taken a pratfall, there has always been a helping hand to get him back on his wobbly feet. Likewise, there have always been hands on the docks to assist folks in tying up their fishing boats. I had to sell my 26-foot Norwegian trawler several years ago, but if I ever get another one, and I sincerely hope I will, I'm sure there will be people on the docks of Port Washington's beautiful marina to lend a helping hand.

Besides the people who live there, I guess I most love the setting of Port Washington on the shores of Lake Michigan just north of the pier that extends from the marina out into the Big Lake. Accompanied by my dogs – old Arrow and puppy Monty - I walk in the Upper Lake Park on the bluff overlooking the beach every morning for 20 to 30 minutes, depending on the weather. And the view which changes every day is simply amazing. Sometimes the Big Lake is as calm as an inland pond. At other times it can be pounding onto the beach with waves six-foot tall.

Sometimes I take my dogs for a walk on the beach. If the weather is fair we walk all the way north to the so-called "Mile Rock" and back to the car parked by the sewage treatment plant. (No it does not smell!) I imagine that this huge rock got its name from the distance between it and the city hall. I reckon that my walk from the parking lot to the Rock and back would also cover about a mile. That's got to be one of the most pleasant miles on the face of Planet Earth. Take my word for it, sports fans!

Q is for Quince Tree

Trees are important objects in our lives, because, I suppose, of their permanence. Like the solitary quince tree that spread its gnarled branches in our backyard, neighborhoods had deep roots and never changed. Except for one rental property, all residents were permanent homeowners. In the first 17 years of my stay here on Planet Earth the homes on the two blocks of Elizabeth Street in Battle Creek, Michigan, never changed hands. My father, a skilled softball catcher, organized an annual Upper versus Lower block softball game, and the lineups never changed, because nobody ever moved. Why would they? Their jobs were within a five-minute drive, or even walking distance. Elementary (Fremont) school was just four blocks away. W.K. Kellog.Junior High School and Battle Creek Central High School were just a mile away, less if you took a couple of short cuts through parks.

All this changed after World War II. In the twenty years after the war, only a handful of the homes on Elizabeth Street were still occupied by their pre-war owners. I would not dare to judge whether the loss of neighborhood stability was necessarily a bad thing. Let's just say that there were many things that, in retrospect, I liked about the permanence of the old-fashioned neighborhoods. (In my action-packed life, I experienced 25 permanent changes of address in a dozen countries on three continents.) Though I have no regrets about any of these moves, I have to admit that it's mighty nice to sit back and enjoy the annual blooming of the big dogwood tree in my backyard and take my dogs on runs in the Upper Lake Park overlooking Lake Michigan twice a day.

Now what in all creation does this have to do with quince trees. Well, believe it or not there is a connection. Like changes of address, the quince fruit imparts an especially fresh, tart flavor to life. Both of my parents loved the little quince tree that grew all alone in our backyard. It was the only growing thing that my Dad, who grew up on a farm in Hickory Corners, Michigan, could care for in the way that he cared for crops during his childhood.

One day when I drove into our driveway I saw him sitting quietly on a folding lawn chair by the driveway at the back of our house. He was contemplating his little quince tree, maybe thinking back to his youth spent among all the growing things on the family farm in Hickory Corners. That was before his father sold the farm and moved his family into the Calhoun County seat in Marshall, Michigan, where he set about his second career as a cabinet maker in a workshop behind the main house. I still have a softball bat and a chest of drawers which Grandpa Goodrich fashioned by his own hands. These presents created out of cherry wood by the loving hands of my grandfather are family keepsakes, which will one day be used by my grandsons – Paul and Phillip Lance Goodrich. I trust that they will treasure these gifts handcrafted by their great grandfather as much as I have.

R is for Race

I guess I didn't really think about race in my childhood. There wasn't any reason to, because in my neighborhood there was only one race. On the north side of town in Battle Creek, Michigan, we were white. In fact, the only person we knew with a different skin color was Pat the Mailman, and he was very simply one of the most loved human beings in our lives. Even our dogs loved Pat perhaps because he loved them in the same way he loved us neighborhood kids, who kept him company on his rounds.

Pat was a big man with a big body and a big voice who at once commanded respect and exuded love for everyone in the neighborhood he served so well during his long life of service. He was family.

In junior high school (grades 7 through 9) named after the city's largest employer W.K. Kellogg, I became schoolmates with a few negroes, but never became close friends with any until high school when I played on football teams with several black teammates. I still recall playing beside an all-state end named Charles Lett, who later served as a respected member of the Battle Creek police department. It was in college after the war that I first came into close contact with several African-American students with whom I served in a political science club. One of the members of the club and I became real buddies and I still recall with pleasure the hours we spent studying for final exams over coffee at the (then all-male) Michigan Union cafeteria. (Today if one lingers in the cafeteria for more than a few minutes, he'll be asked to drink up and move out to make room for other paying customers.) His name was Hesper Jackson, and he was a smart little guy with a great sense of humor who lived in Detroit. I recall an incident that happened while Hesper and I were having a beer in a Columbus, Ohio, hotel bar during a Big Ten political science conference there. After serving us, the bartender noisily started making a big fuss washing glasses. I called out and asked him if he had a problem serving me and my friend. He responded: "No, not at all, it's just a quarrel I had with my boss this morning."

In a few moments, Hesper took me by the arm and whispered "Thanks for asking him." I suddenly realized the pain that my close friend must have felt as a result of being unable to plead his own cause, lest he be viewed as *uppity*.

At one meeting of our club I got into a dispute with another Negro member, a big man whose name I can't recall, who embraced radical Marxist views of the world.. In a heated argument with him I had lost my temper and called him a "dumb sonuvabitch." Now that was a pretty dumb thing for me to do, since he could have broken my face and thrown me out the door with one hand. Instead, he responded to my rude remark with a smile as warm as the sun, and a bear hug that nearly crushed my ribcage. I only later came to understand that this man's impulsive response to my rude remark was an act of loving gratitude for my treating him as simply a friend. We had bonded as brothers, and to this day I thank him for demonstrating to me how important it must be for all kinds of minorities to be accepted for whom and what they are: brothers and sisters under a loving God, rather than as persons requiring special consideration to purge their white brothers of their inappropriate, yea insulting, sense of guilt.

S is for Sammy

On November 11, 1990, a late-sleeping sun slowly rose on the horizon overlooking the Community Hospital in Menomonee Falls, Wisconsin, to shine down on the birth of Samantha Helen Stender Goodrich. The eyes of her father, who had earlier witnessed the birth of two daughters and two sons, filled with joyful tears. The miracle of life never lost its magic. Mona, her mother, took Sammy into her arms for the first of a million hugs before returning the infant to the nurse.

Sammy spent her early years on her mother's family homestead in Hubertus, Wisconsin, in the beautiful rolling hills of the Kettle-Moraine landscape sculpted by ancient glaciers in the heartland of America. It was a great place to grow up, with a 100-year old Macintosh apple tree to climb and old chinked-log barn buildings, one of which her Daddy used to do his writing an as an office, to play in. After a few years, however, Sammy outgrew the boundaries of her rural surroundings as she prepared for a role on a bigger stage. Maybe happy visits with her parents to places in Western Europe encased in the warm memories of *their* younger days strengthened and expanded her world's horizons. Wherever her cosmopolitan genes came from, she clearly possessed from early childhood a keen appreciation of the world stage onto which she was born.

She felt right at home climbing around in ancient fortresses in Ireland and Scotland, where American tourists clamored to take pictures of this "typical lassie" to take back and show to their friends in the States.

Sammy demonstrated at an early age an acute interest in and love of the theatre. Although there is no evidence that Mona played an active role in supporting her daughter's pursuit of a career on the stage, the record speaks for itself. In Port Washington High School, where singing and acting have long boasted exceptionally strong programs, Sammy appeared in a dozen productions to get off to a fast start as a music/theatre major at the University of Wisconsin – Milwaukee. Her early roles included Mrs. Paroo in *Music Man*; Mrs. Potts in *Beauty and the Beast*; Mama Morton in *Chicago*; Dottie in *Noises Off!*; and Reno Sweeney in *Anything Goes*. In her first years in college, Sammy played the Captain in *Starboard Bound*; Rose in *Unity*; Sister Hannah in *As It Is In Heaven*; and Pauline in *No, No Nanette*.

Break a leg, Sammy!

S is for Sex and Secrecy – Birds of a Feather

Yes, sports fans, there is definitely a linkage between sex and secrecy. That's what provides espionage with its seminal appeal. It's a big reason why those of us who chose life in the world of shadows stuck with careers whose only recognition would come in the form of personal satisfaction derived from patriotic service. Persons who devote their lives to working secretly to provide intelligence information vital to our national security are not awarded medals until after they're buried. While public recognition must be withheld so long as he or she lives, the CIA covert operations officer might also find it impossible to gain employment in the private sector after his retirement. In my case, the cover I used for most of my career as a free-lance journalist was exposed by a person seeking to avenge career wrongs he felt he had suffered at the hands of a one-time boss. After he alleged my use of journalist cover, it was impossible for me to get employment in the media after I retired from government service. I was frozen out of the job market, left out in the cold, much like the victims of Senator McCarthy's witch hunts that had transpired many years before. I suppose that those of us who committed ourselves to a life of secrecy were a special breed of people, for whom public recognition is neither sought nor needed. Still and all, like sex, secrecy provides life out of public view its own special satisfactions. Like when my hotel room buzzer sounded at noon I opened the door dressed only in my under shorts wiping shaving cream residue from my face.

After letting my visitor in, I apologized for my attire with a lame explanation about of having had a late evening recuperating from a bumpy trans-Atlantic flight from New York. Actually my travel to the hotel took less than an hour, but my explanation served a dual purpose: it made it appear that my meeting with him was sufficiently important to warrant a trans-Atlantic flight, and it set the stage for a meeting of some considerable duration. (This impression was reinforced by the appearance on the coffee table of an array of delectable luncheon sandwiches). Another advantage to my state of semi-nakedness – and I must confess I had not thought of this at the time – was that it demonstrated to my guest that I was unarmed.

I introduced myself as a special U.S. government intelligence official assigned to obtain accurate information on the intentions of the Castro regime. (I quickly flashed a phony identification card, which I knew would carry little if any credence to my pitch). Much of the information we received, I lamented, came from exile sources with a vested interest in coloring their reports to support their particular anti-Castro views. He agreed wholeheartedly, and we were immediately joined in a common purpose, the essential element of any successful recruitment approach. The meeting lasted a couple of hours and when we parted with a place, date and time set for a second meeting, at a secret site closer to his home (and mine), it was understood that he had joined in a conspiratorial relationship with a secret agency of the U.S. government to achieve the goals that had brought him into the revolutionary movement several years before. He was not betraying the patriotic objectives which had propelled him into a revolutionary cause several years before but rather was taking a different and more challenging course to achieve the noble goals of the Revolution by working against his former communist associates who had betrayed them. This may appear to be an academic distinction, but it was the key to my recruitment of penetration agents inside our enemy's soft underbelly.

T is for Timo

My youngest child, like the three who preceded him was born overseas. I generally explain this geographical fact as the result of my being unable to afford the cost of hospital care and physicians services in the United States. Actually it resulted from the fact that my career required me to spend more time living abroad than in the U.S. of A. The youngest of the four children born to Austin and Eva Goodrich came into this world in Holland, aka the Netherlands. He was born with a sunny smile on his face and kept it in place forever after.

The first – and last – problem with Timo was his name. His Mom and I both favored short names so that our children would not be saddled with poly-syllable, more or less unpronounceable given names, which often led to the imposition of rude, crude or slangy nicknames with which the child might be stuck for life. In line with this rule, we decided to name our second boy *Timo*. This is a fairly common name in Finland, where our first boy child had been born. Unfortunately, in the Netherlands the name of an infant had to be accepted by the state authorities before the birth cold be formally recorded. Most of the names given to Dutch babies were a mile long and included at least one, usually several, names from the Bible; e.g., Cornelius, abbreviated to Kees.

We finally settled on naming our second son Timothy, which in practice was later shortened to Timo. It's been a good name for him – phonetically spelled, easy to remember, hard to forget.

Timo was given a middle name taken from the first name of one of my closest friends, Lancelot , aka *Lance*, Keyworth. Lance ran a translation agency in Helsinki, Finland, and served as the Finnish correspondent of Time-Life magazine and the Financial Times of London. He was married to the widow of a Finnish Army officer who was a 1936 Olympic 5,000 meter distance runner. Giving his name to serve as my son's middle name proved prophetical. Like Lance Keyworth, Timothy Lance Goodrich was imbued with abiding love of family, friends and the core Christian values embodied in the Ten Commandments. Though most of us embrace these behavioral guideposts in name, few of us are able to live by them as consistently or as well as my young son, Timothy Lance Goodrich.

Unlike many members of his generation, Timo entered into a career and stuck with it. It started with a course in welding, which I suggested Timo sign up for in Cleveland. It became his career and he became very good at it. He started work in northern Virginia and later took his work to Chicago where he became a foreman in Ironworkers Local 1. The Big One as it's known, became Timo's professional home and served as a rock solid employment home base. His marriage to his high school sweetheart, Didi, proved less stable, as she was unable to cope with the problem of booze, though she brought into this world three wonderful children: two sons (Phillip, who served two tours in the Marines, and Paul, who followed in his dad's footsteps as a Local 1 Ironworker) and a red-headed daughter, Jordan, who lives and works in Florida.

Timo remarried to a published writer and English teacher named Molly Moynahan, and the two have enjoyed a happy life in a fine apartment on the top floor of a high-rise building with a magnificent skyline view of the *Windy City* of Chicago.

T is for Tina

Like her older sister, Britt Vesla Goodrich, Tina was born with red hair in Stockholm, the capital city of Sweden. That's where the similarity between these sisters came to an end, at least on the surface, and that's probably a good thing. (Wouldn't it be boring if siblings were born with identical personalities?) While Britt entered our universe quietly wearing a contented smile, her kid sister came in with a scream that shook rafters at Almaenna BB Hospital in Stockholm. Once when I came in for a visit, I heard an ear-splitting scream that echoed through the lobby of the hospital like a a subway train bursting out of the Holland tunnel under the Hudson River. A nurse passing by looked at me, nodded her head and said, "Ja, she's yours."

While Tina had the louder voice, her older sister generally played the leading role in the close-knit lives of these wonderful girls. One summer afternoon in the wooded back yard at the top of the hill on Hane St. in McLean, Virginia, I looked out of the kitchen window to see Britt feeding her trusting kid sister an angle worm. A few years later, I happened to come home late to our red brick three-story house in Scheveningen (near the Peace Palace in The Hague), to see Tina stretched out on the attic rooftop retrieving a bottle of Coke from its hiding place on the next door neighbor's rain gutter. Britt was there, of course, securely holding onto her kid sister's ankles!

But it took more than a big sister to keep those feet from moving. After two years at Mary Washington College in Fredriksburg, VA, near our home, Tina expressed a wish to transfer to a larger school. I said I would only go that more expensive route if she wanted to major in studies there that were not available in Virginia. Well, the little rascal found that her lifetime academic goal in line with her experience living abroad was to major in Scandinavian studies. So it was *On, Wisconsin!* After which, Tina spent a summer in sunny Oslo, Norway working as a waitress in a coffee shop on KarlJohan St..

After graduation, Tina moved home and applied for a job at CIA. Months passed as the security clearance process ground slowly forward. Meanwhile, she was offered a job working for a small newspaper chain in rural Virginia. Tired of waiting for her CIA clearance, Tina asked my advice and I said take the newspaper job, mainly because there were few professional opportunities for women in CIA in those days. It was a good move, as she went from reporting to public relation to become a top executive in the International Design Institute of America. Happily married to Bill Rollins, Tina retired early with time to devote to raising her two wonderful daughters: Lilly, a University of Arizona college grad and her flute-playing high school sister, Rosie.

Tina doesn't climb out of third-story bedroom windows to retrieve Coke bottles anymore. Nor does she cut her hand breaking into a locked front door when she's forgotten her house key as she once did in Helsinki. But don't be surprised if she one day reappears on the masthead of a major media publication because she's still highly energetic, creative and as smart as a whip. She's my beloved Teena-beana.

T is for Tina Remembers

by Kristina Goodrich

Editorial Note: I asked my second-borne daughter, Kristina Goodrich, aka Tina, to write a few spontaneous recollections that appear in the rear view mirror of *her* life. Here's what she came up with - a slice of *Tinarama* (Keep refrigerated).

Dad dragged us all over the world, and what do I remember?

The Food. We relished Indonesian in Holland, pizza in Germany and Chinese in Bangkok, where we bought from the ding-a-ling man who biked around every afternoon with his glass cases full of chopped sugar cane and very tart guavas, which he'd cut with a sharp cleaver while turning the fruit in his hand. I wondered that he still had all his fingers! Then he'd put the fruit in a paper cone, we'd pay him a few baht (a few pennies) and walk away happy, knowing that this was precious food we'd never see again. And he'd ride off, no antibacterial products to burden his biking or his bottom line. Hey, Mama had survived scraping the inside of a banana peel she found on the street in occupied Norway during World War II. We all assumed that we could do the same.

The Travel. Dad gave us marvelous cultural experiences that have enriched my life, if not my college entrance applications. But, while he'd always be there to greet us at our foreign destinations, he'd never participate in the packing. In our 1964 move from Oslo to the States, Mama had to pack rough-and-tumble clothes for our vacation in the mountains of Norway, dressy clothes for our First Class travel across the Atlantic aboard the Norway-America Lines *Stavangerfjord* and hot weather clothes for our first few months of *temporary* lodging in tropical northern Virginia. Were we kids any help in our dozens of inter-continental moves? Heavens no! Once, Britt added the final dollop to Mama's travel exhaustion by deciding that she really didn't want to leave [Norway], she really liked it here and she was absolutely not leaving again to *anywhere*. I found her on a steep slope behind our house crying, her hands over her eyes. I could feel her pain and certainly sympathized but I had also seen the despair in Mama's eyes. Britt was spitting into the wind of our ineluctable fate. I guess the spit hit her and she realized the futility of her rebellion. She came along, which made me happy because she was my best friend and best playmate and best advisor.

The Lodging. Always the best! First Class across the Atlantic four times that I remember. And the hotels! A top-floor suite in Hong Kong that featured one bedroom, three parlors a dining room and *seven* bathrooms.

In Beirut, en route to Bangkok, we arrived exhausted at the Pan Am hotel at midnight. (Daddy had left earlier, taking the trans-Pacific route to Thailand.) Mama and I opted for the restaurant, but Britt, Jay and Timo wanted room service. Remembering the size of fast-foot hamburgers at home, they ordered two each. The burgers arrived, each seven inches across! Someone ate most of that dinner that was placed in the hall, but it was certainly not my siblings. We still laugh about it.

And then the Fairmont in San Francisco. Wow! Gorgeous, huge rooms, which Britt and I got to occupy with our brothers while Mom and Dad went out on the town to enjoy the night life with the Muldoons, CIA Station comrades and friends of ours in Bangkok. Not fair, we thought, but it was hard to be miserable amid such luxury!

The Illness. Thank heavens for the inventon of penicillin. Neither Britt nor I would have survived without it. On top of measles, German and domestic, chicken pox and mumps (for none of which vaccines were yet invented), I managed to acquire a variety of other illnesses. I recall how the pretty little dresses hanging in a closet next to my bed in the Helsinki Childrens' hospital provided a strong incentive to get well so I could put them on and get out of bed to play with the other kids. Once when Dad visited this hospital and complimented my doctor on the care they provided, he was taken to the lounge where photos of the staff adorned the walls. My doctor pointed out that every member of the staff had received training at U.S. medical colleges paid for by the interest on Finland's repayment of WW I loans. (This made me very proud of my country.)

In Holland as in Finland, hospitalized children were got out of bed as soon as possible. When I was five years old and recovering from a kidney illness in The Hague, Netherlands, I shared a room with a five year old who had been hit by a bus. She was covered with bandages and did not move much. But I knew I could fix that. I let her rest a day and then I was out of the crib and pretended to be her nurse, though she must have found it odd to have at her side a red-headedd sprite spouting a multi-lingual mix of Swedish, Norwegian, Dutch and English. Alas, there came a day when I didn't love her. I was put on a liquid-free diet, which featured crackers, crackers and a few more crackers all without salt. Of course that was the day that a loving relative delivered to my roomate a huge basket of fruit. Can you imagine how good that fruit looks when you've eaten nothing but dry food for five housrs? I whined, I pleaded, I cried. But no fruit did I get. Bah!

For some reason, one of my vividest memories of illness is that it was a good thing to be sick. Mama and Dad made it that way. Once Dad asked me if there was anything he could do to make me feel better, and I slyly admitted that there had been this doll…. Mama had her own reward system. She let us stay in bed when we were sick. Now Mama and Dad had two twin beds shoved together, but it was always on Mama's side that I lay. And she would even let me wash my Sonny Boy doll in a basin on the bed, which wet the eider down comforter and sheets despite plentiful towels. And then the doctor would come and give me a shot and let me keep the medicine vial to play with. It was so much more fun to play doctor with his real things than those plastic toy devices in toy doctor bags.

It's funny what we most clearly remember. I have few memories of holidays, birthdays. I don't recall much of the history and culture of the places where I lived. But what touched me personally, like the food, the travel and illnesses, was that even in the harder times there was love and joy!

T is for Travel with Nonne

I suppose I've traveled more than most folks, thanks to numerous study and career assignments in Europe and Southeast Asia, but the month I spent traveling in Western Europe with my sister Eleanor (aka Nonne) in the summer of 1948 stands out in my mind as the most as memorable journey of all. The year was historically pivotal in marking the onset of the Cold War and the emergence of the United States as the major super power of the free world. We encountered this post WW II reality head on.

We started our month in Europe by taking the overnight boat trip from Stockholm to Turku on the west coast of Finland where we boarded the train bound for Helsinki. An hour before reaching the Finnish capital we encountered the iron curtain, quite literally, in the form of steel shutters bolted up over the windows to prevent our seeing the naval base in Porkkala which the Finns had been forced to lease to the Soviets at the end of WW II. (When the Finns got the territory back 20 years later, they had to demolish the Russian military housing, which was declared unfit for human habitation.)

In Helsinki the mood was grim as the Communist popular front party campaigned to install a communist-led government as had happened in Czechoslovakia a few months before. We witnessed at first hand how Hertta Kuusinen, whose father was a member of the Politburo in Moscow, implored huge market square crowds to bring communists into power via the ballot box. It was a crucial crossroads. Despite huge Soviet pressure, Finnish voters turned out in record numbers to maintain their parliamentary democracy free of communist domination.

Next stop, wonderful Copenhagen, where there was no hot water at the hotel, but I was able to sell my damaged typewriter for twice its value. Nonne sold her nylon stockings, which provided us with spending money for a week. (If she had brought a dozen pair along we could have lived like royalty for a month.)

Onward to the U.S. occupation zone in Frankfurt, West Germany. After living off the rest of Europe for years, Germany was financially and spiritually broken in defeat. Old men picked cigarette butts up off the street and piles of rubble remained in the street outside the ghostly skeletons of bombed out buildings. On a Sunday a few days after we arrived, Minister of Economics Gerhardt pulled off an economic miracle by simply issuing new currency and ending all rationing. On Monday morning the market places overflowed with goods and shoppers and the whole country rocketed into prosperity. It was an unbelievable material transformation that happened before our eyes over night.

Our train from Frankfurt am Main got about half way to Rome when we were halted in Arrezo, Tuscany by a general strike called by the powerful Italian communist party after someone shot Italian Communist leader Palmiro Togliatti. We chartered a taxi driver to take us to Rome, but were stopped after an hour by group of communists armed with sub-machineguns who let us understand that no travel was permitted until further notice, since the communist party was shutting down the country. Their authority was vested in submachine guns slung over their shoulders. So we agreed to return to witness a triumphant Communist parade through the streets of Arrezo. We then bribed a railroad official to move us from our crowded, hot and sweaty 3rd class coach seats into a 1st class compartment to complete our trip to the capital city of Italy.

Our onward journey into France was uneventful except for one slight inconvenience. While we slept, someone lightened our baggage by removing our large suitcase from the rack over our heads. This left us to travel for ten days in the clothes on our backs, which for Eleanor included a New Look (unseen in Europe at that time) raincoat. Nonne's fiancée (and later husband), Bob Guilbert, wired money he had borrowed from his boss, NBC's Today show host, Dave Garroway. Nonne went from rags to riches, dressed in a hand-tailored linen suit created in a fashion shop near the Madelaine Church on the Rue Tronchet.

Crossing the English Channel, we quickly discovered that the 1948 Olympics were just started in London and there were no hotel room available in the city a week before the sailing date of our ship, the Queen Elizabeth from Southampton. Forunately, Mother had given Nonne the telephone number of the English Speaking Union, provided bv an old Wells College roommate, to call if we needed help in Merry olde England. This led us to the doorstep of Lady Spender Clay's estate (most of which was now taken over by a divinity school) on the emerald moors of Kent, where as her house guests we worked with her gardener for nearly a week before she bid us farewell with some pounds in wages to catch our ship home. The Lady gave us a memorable glimpse of the quality that stamped the English aristocracy. A sneak peak in her guest book revealed the names of everyone who was anyone in England, including members of the royal family. The lands of the estate had been confiscated by the state and leased to a divinity school, her domestic staff of dozens had been reduced to a maid and a gardener, but not once did this Lady utter a single word of complaint. *That's* class.

We concluded our trip past the Statue of Liberty viewed through the teary eyes of European war refugees en route to a new life in the New World. The Statue of Liberty took on a new and lasting depth of meaning for us. When we returned to our beloved family home at 38 Elizabeth St., we were embraced by our loving parents. We hugged them tightly and silently thanked God – *for the birds that sing - and for everything.*

T is for Terror

I suppose that fear is a rather common human condition with which we have to learn to cope in our lives. For many of us our first experience with this deep-seated emotion may arise in connection with simply getting lost. I recall how I somehow got separated from my parents and siblings during a vacation trip aboard a tourist ferry boat from Detroit to a Lake Erie beach in Ohio. (It must have been in the early 1030's when I was five or six years old, because I recall that it happened on the morning after Joe Louis had knocked out the Italian heavyweight Primo Carnera to the raucous cheers of black crew members gathered around a radio set in the purser's office. I could *feel* their excitement as the Brown Bomber ushered black pride into American society with a crushing left hook.)

The next morning I somehow I became separated from the rest of my family and I remember the panic I felt at being lost. That was terror.

A dozen years later I lay at the base of a fir tree on a German hillside under *friendly* fire grasping for cover and praying, yea, shouting, for God to make 'em stop! "Please God. Please make 'em stop!" That, too, was terror.

Once on an operational trip into France to attempt to recruit a French Communist Party member with connections in Moscow, I was held up by a customs official who demanded to inspect my toilet articles kit. In it he discovered an envelope in which I had carelessly placed my true name identification papers. He quickly observed my picture on a true name document different from the name on the travel document I had just shown him. I felt a momentary pang - terror. But before he had a chance to act on his suspicion that I might be traveling under a false name, I grabbed the envelope from his hand, jammed it back into my bag, nodded and proceeded on my way with a brief "Merci, monsieur!" I suspected that petty officials acting like bullies could be themselves bullied, and I was right. But it was the last time I failed to conceal my false name identification papers in the concealment compartment in my brief case.

U is for Underground

When our English cousins with whom we share a different language speak of the *underground*, they're referring to a mode of mass transit, what we Americans call the subway. We Yanks use underground to describe any activity that takes place in secret, outside the public domain. In government usage, information classified as confidential, restricted, secret or top secret refers to information that comes from a source, whose identity needs to be concealed from public view. Why does the identity of the source of classified information need to be kept secret? Well, to protect him or her from embarrassment or worse - much worse. The code of silence of the Mafia brotherhood, for example, was – and probably still is – enforced by the death penalty. You talk to our enemies – the police – about who we are and what we do – you end up in the Hudson River wearing a concrete kimono.

I worked underground (i.e., under non-official cover) for about twenty years, which may not be a world record but my cover certainly held up longer than most. There is no denying that the use of non-official employment cover has the advantages for the government of plausible denial. For example, if a farmer in Finland one day accidentally uncovers a cache of secret radio equipment buried by me for use by secret agent networks in the event of World War III, the U.S. Government can deny having had anything to do with it. There are no markings on the equipment that would make it possible to identify its American origin. Of course that protection does not extend to the agent, me. In the unlikely event that I was caught in the act of burying secret radio equipment, I'd have faced a fine, imprisonment or both. But that's just a risk that goes with the job.

By the same token, if a person whom I attempted to recruit to provide secret information to the U.S. government reported my effort to authorities in that country, I'd be subject to expulsion or imprisonment. That's just one of the risks that the CIA employee takes when he signs up to serve his country working in the shadows, sometimes as a primary target of our country's enemies. It is nasty work, without public recognition or great material benefits, but somebody has got to do it. And I have to say that from my the experience, the intangible rewards of patriotic service in the field of espionage match or exceed the benefits of any other profession, whether inside the government or anywhere else.

V is for Vestmannagatan and Vikstenvaegen

These streets in Stockholm that could be translated into English as Western Man St. and Harbor Stone Rd. were the first residences I established in the capital of Sweden in 1948-49. Little did I know then what a pivotal role this city and life abroad would play in my life after World War II.

Vestmannagatan was a downtown residential street a few blocks from the campus of Stockholms Hoegskollan where I had enrolled to complete my third college year under the G.I. Bill of Rights. How did I happen to apply to take my third year of college at a school in a country with which I had had no previous connection, no blood relatives or academic interest? Well, I guess my feet were itching (a condition that persisted for the next three decades) and I wanted to get out into the world that combat service in WW II had gotten me into. The absence of any rational motivation for my decision to study in Sweden led to so many probing questions that I decided to explain my move by adopting a fictional Swedish grandmother. End of questions. I had Swedish blood in my veins, which explained everything to everyone's satisfaction..

It was challenging to live in Western Europe in those days. Except for very young people who were raised on American jazz, almost nobody in Sweden spoke English and menus were in Swedish only. It was learn Swedish or die and I had no intention of ending my visit on planet Earth in 1948, so I learned Swedish in about eight weeks with study in school supplemented with long, pleasurable hours on the *horizontal dictionary*. One of my teachers was "Kitty," a divorced baroness with two sons, who lived a twenty-five minute bus drive away on the south side of Stockholm. Kitty and I were separated after she had an operation and I explained that I could not get married before finishing college. I only got together with Kitty on one other occasion, but she will forever remain a warm memory of love from the cold winter of 1947-48.

Vikstensvaegen 60 in the post WWII suburb of Gaerdet was a two-bedroom apartment, which I was able to rent at a price that my GI Bill monthly stipend of $60 would cover. I shared the place with Harold "Sam" Haight, from Redlands, CA, who had served as a naval officer in the war. Sam dated Eva Hvronkova, a gorgeous blonde student from Czechoslovakia who one day got a pivotal letter from her father saying that her homeland was being taken over by the communists and that she must stay abroad. (I can't imagine how painful that letter must have been for him to write.) Sam asked for my advice and I told him that if he didn't marry Eva, he'd regret it the rest of his life. He was happy to have his intention confirmed and the couple promptly got married. They've lived happily ever after in southern California and overseas where Sam served with the Agency for International Development. Included in their travels have been several visits with Eva's family in Czechoslovakia, which managed to free itself from the shackles of communist control with the dissolution of the Soviet Empire that came to be named the Prague Spring after Eva's birthplace.

W is for Wolverines

You'll never see a wolverine being paraded on a leash around the football field at the Big House in Ann Arbor. That's because this little 30-inch long 40 pound member of the weasel family is pound-for-pound the toughest and meanest of God's creations. He's been known to gnaw off a leg to get out of a trap. He also happens to be the mascot of my beloved University of Michigan football team and *that* is why I love him.

I suppose that I inherited my love of my father's college, the University of Michigan. Cyrus J. Goodrich went through the U of M Law School (class of '19) after teaching school in the Michigan Upper Peninsula to raise money to pay for college. After the war, when I expressed interest in possibly following in his footsteps, my father took me to see the Dean of the Law School, who said that I'd be able to skip the four years of pre-law education and go straight into the great Michigan Law School if that's what I wanted. After prayerful consideration of this generous offer, I finally decided to stay in the Literature, Science and the Arts program leading to a Bachelor of Arts degree and some sort of career in world affairs. Maybe I lacked the motivation or the courage, to go straight into Law School with the goal of following in my father's footsteps, to practice law and to spend the rest of my life in Battle Creek, Michigan. Maybe I wanted something a little bit bigger, a little bit more challenging. (Well, I certainly found *that* working for 25 years as a staff officer, mostly under deep cover, in the Central Intelligence Agency.)

My first experience in the Big House in Ann Arbor that holds more than 110,000 fans was as a Boy Scout usher. Yes, in the mid-1930's our Scout troop in Battle Creek supplied ushers for fans attending Michigan football games in the U of M stadium. (This practice was later discontinued, probably because of some sort of liability issue.) Anyway, a half century later I was back in the stadium and I met a visiting fan from the University of Iowa. We struck up a conversation and I told him how as a Boy Scout usher, I had seen the University of Iowa gridiron great Nile Kinnick, who was killed in WWII, play on ths field.

"My God!" he exclaimed to his companion, "This man saw Nile Kinnick play here in this stadium, on this football field." It was as if he had just learned that I had seen Jesus Christ walk on water. "My God, said his Cornhusker companion, "let me shake your hand, sir"

I smiled and graciously extended my hand.

Well, I'm still a diehard Wolverine fan, and I still go to watch my beloved Michigan football team engage in heroic struggles on this field. But changes are in the offing. They're going to install heated box seats now so you can watch the Wolverines play in air-conditioned comfort. Well, not me. Football, *real* football, is played outdoors in the cold. And if you're a fan, a real fan, you're going to freeze your ass off watching the game. Why? Because it's Michigan football, not tiddlywinks.

X Marks the Spot

It seems funny when I think about it now. But it was serious business on my first overseas tours of duty as as staff agent with the CIA in the early 1950's. I had been trained in how to bury radio sets and signal plans in the ground for use by secret agents in the early stages of a third world war. Now it was time to put my training into practice.

Together with an agent, an amateur radio "ham," I drove out into the heavily wooded forest of Finland in the middle of the night and buried radio sets wrapped in waterproof packages. I drew a map to pinpoint their exact locations so they could be dug up and used by secret agents in the event of WW III. (Earlier, to support unilateral stay-behind nets in Sweden I had I had signed up an agent to act as custodian of a secret cache of gasoline to be used by stay-behind agents.)

At a meeting in London of case officers from other countries working to establish stay behind networks in the event of WW III, I felt proud that my assets though few in number were all controlled directly and exclusively by CIA. Other stations reported on plans for huge stay behind networks, but their operations were shared with agencies of other countries and, thus, were not subject to our direct control. Not only did we have to agree with our partners on when to activate these nets, but their security was handled by the secret services of countries beyond our control. At a Stay-behind ops conference in London I was at first embarrassed by the modest size of my handful of assets, but I came to be proud of the fact that the security and control of my nets rested exclusively in CIA hands. Thank God we never had to activate these plans. Thank God that World War III never happened.

Y is for Young Christian Sites
for Men and Women

Y was the single letter designation of two places that played important roles in my high school experience in Battle Creek, Michigan. The first place was the Young Men's Christian Association, which was a renovated old Victorian residence on Capital Avenue, named for the fact that, as M78, it linked the state capital cities of Lansing, Michigan, and Indianapolis, Indiana. I'm not sure what the main purpose was of the old white framed Victorian dwelling, but an upstairs great room served as a sort of informal workout room for young men. There were bar bells, a stationary bicycle and a squared ring surrounded by worn grey ropes that qualified it for use as a place to train aspirant young men boxers. Though I can't recall that I ever signed up as a member of the YMCA association, I was happy to work out there occasionally in the company of a high school friend named "Happy" Harpster.

Happy, who was a grade ahead of me in school, was also a traveling companion on summer hitch-hiking excursions to the Lake Michigan resort city of Ludington together with a younger friend named Jim Buchanan. Jim and I did our best to get Happy, who was old enough at 16 years of age to work without a special permit, to apply for a job at a factory in Lundington so that we could finance our extended stay on the Lake Michigan beaches. Unfortunately, Happy's desire to earn money fell short of our capacity to drink Stroh's beer, and our summer holidays were ended by a lack of hard cash after a week.

It was Happy who introduced me to the joy or working out by lifting weights and boxing at the Y. I liked to box and was more than a match for my high school pals, including older boys John "Demon" Dodge and Jack "Mac" McGregor, both of whom quit sparring with me because of thumb injuries they suffered hitting my hard head. In any case, my boxing career ended when my father refused my request for his permission to enter a junior golden gloves tournament in Battle Creek with the admonition that my mother would not go along with the request.

Physical encounters of quite a different variety took place with members of the opposite sex on the dance floor on Friday evenings at the Young Women's Christian Association (YWCA) located a few blocks closer to downtown on Capitol Avenue. I had been reluctant to join my classmates taking dancing lessons at the Y (as it was called) but came to enjoy these outings in the company of my high school sweetheart, Janet Crowell, a wonderful dancer who lovingly tolerated my lack of expertise on the dance floor. Fortunately, there was little skill involved in dancing to the Big Band jazz of Benny Goodman, Harry James and the Dorsey brothers, Tommy and Jimmy. The step known as the Battle Creek Bounce was like walking with a slight bounce on every third step. (I never got into jitterbugging, though Jan was skilled at the exercise, and I gallantly let her demonstrate her talent with other boys, but not too often or for too long.)

In the summer months after we were old enough to drive cars (age 14), the best place in the world to drink beer and dance on a double date was at the La Belle dance hall attached to the hotel of the same name on beautiful Gull Lake about half way between Battle Creek and Kalamazoo, Michigan. There might be a better place to spend summer weekend evenings but I can't imagine where that might be.

Z is for Zephyr

The Lincoln Zephyr, pride and joy of the Ford Motor Company in the 1940's, was a twelve-cylinder streak of lightning that my speed-loving father could not resist. He bought two of them. The first, a pre-WWII rocket was jade green, the other was a gaudy Indy-500 crimson. Whatever their color those babies could fly, and that's the speed that my dad most enjoyed behind the wheel. Another feature of the Zephyr was a wide cushioned platform under the rear window which exactly fit the configuration of my cocker spaniel dog, Binker, named after an imaginary companion of a young boy by the author A. A. Milne. One summer day in the late forties, Cyrus J. Goodrich, Attorney at Law, drove to his office in the Security National Bank in downtown Battle Creek, Michigan, and parked the car in the basement garage. Eight hours later he drove home and was surprised when Binker climbed down out of his backseat perch to come into the house at 38 Elizabeth Street to join the family for dinner.

Z is for Zippo

The cigarette lighter carried in the side pants pocket of every teen-aged male in the United States from World War II until the end of the century and beyond was called a Zippo. Nobody knew who made this indestructible, indispensable instrument, but if you didn't carry one you were simply written off as a non-smoker or a jerk. Encased in a strong flip-top case made of stainless steel the Zippo without fail produced a large flame with a single flip of the thumb. The only lighter that equaled the Zippo was a brass lighter used by Wehrmacht soldiers in World War II. I used one of these that I had liberated from a German prisoner of war for more than a year. The German lighter that was called a flammenwerfer (flame-thrower) had the advantage of working with ordinary gasoline as fuel. (For all I know the Zippo might have worked with gasoline as well, but nobody ever dared to try this.)

Author Biography

After publication of his first memoir *(Born to Spy; Recollections of a CIA Officer, iUniverse), 2004)*, Austin Goodrich decided to take a second look into his rear-view mirror, where he was surprised to find how much of his life and career in the Central Intelligence Agency had escaped his earlier notice. The result is recorded in these memorabilia, organized alphabetically in the hope of creating some logical order in a shrunken world rent by chaotic change and seemingly irreconcilable conflicts that brought the world's super powers to the brink of mutual extermination. Bon voyage!

CPSIA information can be obtained
at www.ICGtesting.com
Printed in the USA
BVHW030320180120
569564BV00011B/136